TACOMA

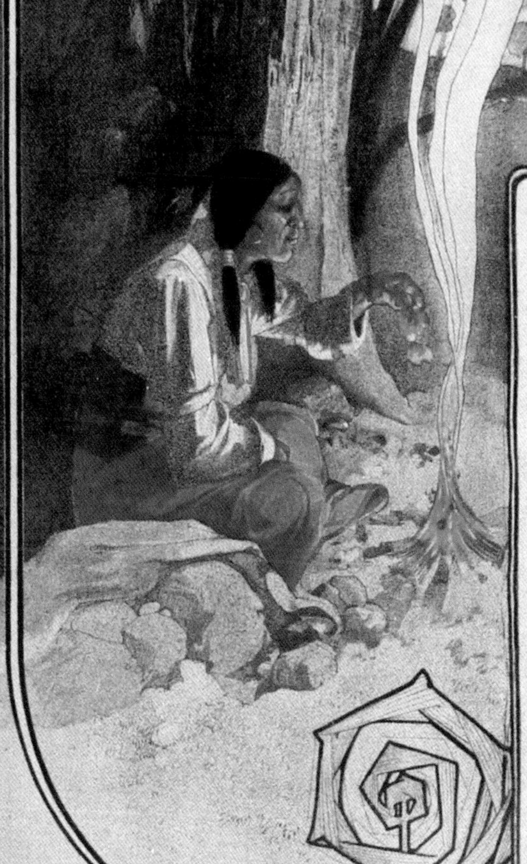

NEW HERALD ANNUAL

1907

PRICE 25 CENTS · THE BELL PRESS PUBLISHERS

SANDERS CO STL

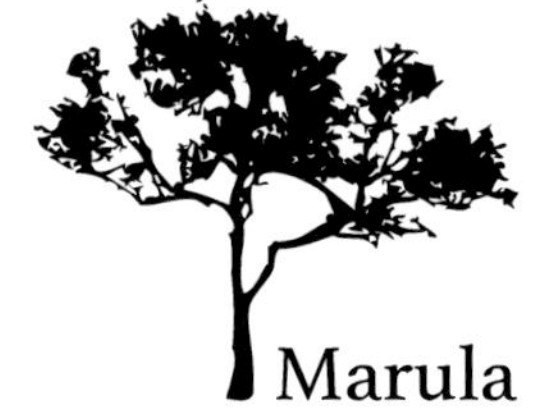

An imprint of Arcadia Publishing

Tacoma New Herald Annual
The Bell Press
T.J. Bell, editor

A Marula Historical Reprint
Originally published in 1907

Published by Arcadia Publishing
Charleston SC

ISBN 978-0-7385-9489-7

Printed in the United States of America

For all general information contact Arcadia Publishing at:
Telephone 843-853-2070
Fax 843-853-0044
E-mail sales@arcadiapublishing.com
For customer service and orders:
Toll-Free 1-888-313-2665

Visit us on the Internet at www.arcadiapublishing.com

Weyerhaeuser Timber Co.

Wholesale Dealers in

Land, Logs and Lumber

General Office, Tacoma, Wash. Mills at Everett, Wash.

THE PUGET SOUND FLOURING MILLS CO.

Manufacturers

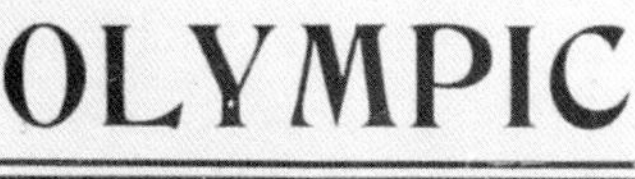

Patent Family Flour
Cake and Pastry Flour
Pancake Flour
Wheat-Hearts

TACOMA - - - WASHINGTON

J. BERGOUST, President. J. E. BURKEE, Vice-President. D. H. BEURHAUS, Secretary.

NORTHWEST CONSERVING CO.

MANUFACTURERS AND PACKERS OF

VINEGAR AND SAUER KRAUT

PICKLES, CATSUP, MUSTARD, HORSERAD-
ISH AND OTHER TABLE CONDIMENTS

Garden City Catsup

IS OUR LEADER, AND HAS MANY FRIENDS

All our goods are fully guaranteed to meet the requirements of the Pure Food Law of the State of Washington.
We solicit your trial order.

FACTORY AND OFFICE
THIRTY-FIRST ST. AND SAWYER AVE. 'PHONE MAIN 345.

Tacoma, Washington

PACIFIC COLD STORAGE CO.

DEALERS AND PACKERS

Frozen, Mild Cured and Canned Salmon, Dressed Meats, Poultry and Perishable Products. Fish Freezing and General Cold Storage. Alaska Trade a Specialty.

N. P. WHARF - - - TACOMA

Cleaning and Dyeing French Dry Cleaning a Specialty

All Work Guaranteed First Class

NEW CITY DYE WORKS

T. H. McCULLOCH, Prop.

730 Pacific Avenue Telephone Main 868

TACOMA, WASHINGTON

LOUIS D. CAMPBELL, *President.*
RALPH METCALF, *Sec. and Treas.*
JOHN L. HARRIS, *General Manager.*

METCALF SHINGLE COMPANY

Established 1894

TACOMA, WASHINGTON

MANUFACTURERS OF

WASHINGTON CEDAR SHINGLES

CEDAR AND FIR LUMBER

The Largest Manufacturers of Red Cedar Shingles. Daily Capacity, Three-Quarters of a Million. Paid-Up Capital, $100,000

MILLS AT KELSO AND CASTLE ROCK, WASH.

J. G. JAEGER, President
G. C. SCHEMPP, Sec'y & Treas.

Tacoma Steam Laundry

INCORPORATED

Prompt Delivery

Pacific Avenue and 26th St. Telephone Main 224

The National Bank of Commerce

TACOMA, WASHINGTON

UNITED STATES DEPOSITARY

Capital, $200,000.00 Surplus, $250,000.00

OFFICERS

CHESTER THORNE, *President.*
ARTHUR F. ALBERTSON, *Vice Pres. and Cashier.*
FREDERICK A. RICE, *Assistant Cashier.*
DELBERT A. YOUNG, *Assistant Cashier.*

DIRECTORS

CHESTER THORNE, *President.*
C. M. LEVEY, *Vice President Northern Pacific Railway Co.*
CHAS. RICHARDSON, *President Pacific Cold Storage Co.*
S. A. PERKINS, *Proprietor News Publishing Co., Ledger Publishing Co.*
A. M. INGERSOLL, *Capitalist.*
WILLIAM JONES, *President Jones-Scott Co.*
W. G. HELLAR, *Broker.*
ARTHUR F. ALBERTSON, *Vice President and Cashier.*

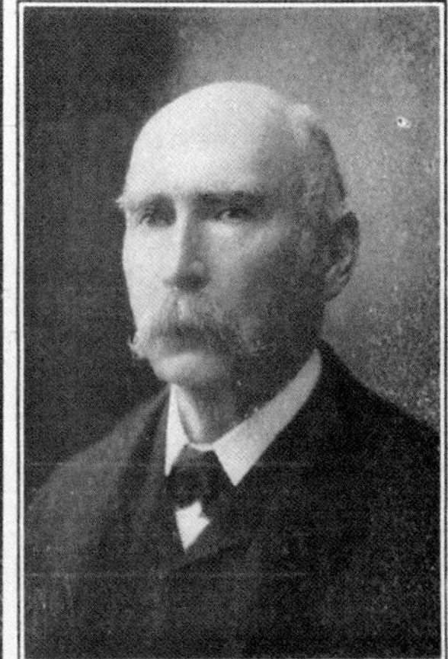

Tel. Black 1807.

Geo. W. Roberts

Manufacturer of and Dealer in

MARBLE AND GRANITE

4726 UNION ST.

Opposite Tacoma Cemetery

SOUTH TACOMA, WASH.

Isaac Pincus & Sons

(Established 1858)

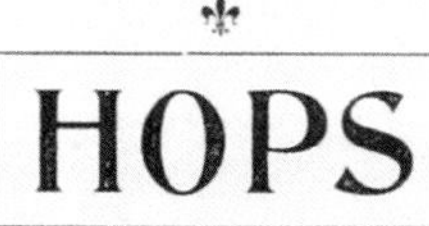

TACOMA, U. S. A.

LINDSTROM & BERG
CABINET MAKERS

CORNER TWENTY-FIRST AND COMMERCE STREETS
TACOMA, WASH.

TELEPHONE MAIN 469

INTERIOR HOUSE WORK IN HARD WOODS

OFFICE, STORE, BANK AND BAR FIXTURES

Office Telephone, Main 474. Residence Telephone, Red 1700

L. A. Nicholson
CIVIL ENGINEER

Platting and Drafting.

Railroad Location and Construction.

SUN AND ELECTRIC BLUE AND BLACK PRINTING.

ROOMS 505-6-7 FIDELITY BUILDING
TACOMA, WASHINGTON.

U. S. and Foreign **PATENTS** And **TRADE MARKS**

R. I. ELLIOTT

313 Fidelity Bldg.,

Tacoma, U. S. A.

DRAWINGS *BLUE PRINTS*

JAMES A. KELLY, E. M. HARRY D. CHAPMAN, C. E.
Telephone James 2601.

KELLY and CHAPMAN
CIVIL AND MINING ENGINEERS

512-13 Provident Building

TACOMA, WASHINGTON, U. S. A.

Surveys, Estimates, Reports, Designing and Superintendence of Construction.

Coal, Iron and Copper Mines, Washing and Coking Plants, Examinations With a View of Decreasing Cost of Operation or Increasing Output, Foundations, Roofs, Bridges, Wharves and Railroad Structures, Water Supply, Drainage, Hydraulic Power Plants, and Railroads and Tramways.

Largest Cigar Factory in the State. Established in 1892.

BEN HAVERKAMP

Manufacturer of HIGH-GRADE HAND-MADE **HAVANA CIGARS**

TACOMA, WASH.

MAKER OF THE POPULAR BRANDS

Flor De Valdez
Absolutely High-Grade Vuelta Abajo Havana Cigar

Olympic
Choice Mild Havana Cigar

State Seal and **Little Duke**
The Old Reliable 5c Sellers

Office and Salesroom, 1104 Pacific Avenue. Factory, Corner Yakima Avenue and Tenth St.

The Quality and Workmanship Represented in My Products are Recognized as the Best by Men Who Know.

McRAE-SHERMAN ELECTRIC CO.

NICHOLS. G. SHERMAN, *Prop.*
Telephone Main 839.

ELECTRICAL ENGINEERS
AND CONTRACTORS

DYNAMOS AND MOTORS. ARMATURE WINDING, HOUSE WIRING, ETC.

1526 COMMERCE ST. - - TACOMA, WASH.

Reliable Automobile Co.

705-707 Pacific Ave.
Garage and Salesrooms

A Thoroughly Equipped and Up-to-Date

Repair Shop

Renting and Supplies

AGENTS FOR

Pope-Toledo, Buick, Oldsmobile, Thomas Cars and Pope-Waverly Electrics

The Tacoma New Herald

THE BELL PRESS, Publishers Established 1891 T. J. BELL, Editor

VOL. 16.—NO. 25 TACOMA, WASH., JANUARY 12, 1907 $1.00 per Year

REASONS WHY

Tacoma Will Be One of the Greatest Cities in America — Counterpart on the Pacific of New York, Jersey City and Philadelphia on the Atlantic

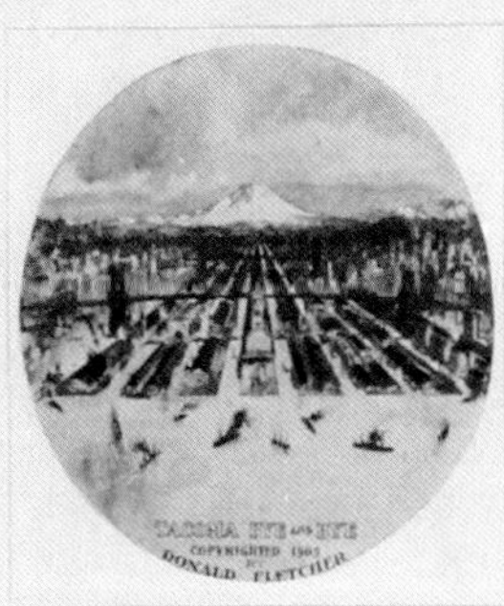

Hon. C. E. Dunkelberger, Lockport, N. Y.: Dear Sir—I have found the place that can become the Greatest City of the World. Hold on there! Laugh if you will AFTER you have read this. The biggest folly is to fool yourself.

The best authorities agree that as to CLIMATIC CONDITIONS, LIFE-SUPPORTING SOIL and WEALTH-PRODUCING LANDS AND WATERS, the Pacific Ocean and lands on each shore half way across the Continent to the Atlantic are more than twice as great and good as those in, and on, the Atlantic half-way across to the Pacific.

When things shall have been "evened up," there will be twice the population bordering on the Pacific that there will then be bordering on the Atlantic.

There is now less than one-tenth of the development of the Pacific that there is of the Atlantic territory.

The great cities of modern times are on level ground or have large bodies of level ground adjacent. This is so because cities live off the mechanics as nations do off the farmers, and mechanics work on level floors or level yards. Every climb up or step down costs money. The same is true of unskilled labor and of transportation. The LEVEL GROUNDS around New York caused it to pass Philadelphia; Chicago to pass Milwaukee and St. Louis; and Minneapolis to pass St. Paul; although in each case THEY WERE SMALLER THAN THEIR RIVALS FOR MANY YEARS. Successful and growing factories require from a few acres to hundreds of acres each, and prefer both rail and water transportation, and must have absolutely level ground. Absence of level lands adjacent to navigable waters, and presence of high hills bankruptive to remove, DOOM A PORT TO CONGESTION AND STAGNATION. From the stand-point of Commerce and Transportation this is pre-eminently true because thousands of acres are required for termini, yard room and warehouses to work the business of a LARGE CITY AND LARGE COMMERCE.

Twenty years ago I reported against investing on Puget Sound, saying that anything above a two-story building was a mistake, because its principal assets were lumber and fish, and only small market for either, and charges then for transportation of those and other products to market were confiscatory. Now rates are lower and markets greater. Annually three billion feet of lumber is cut (from the two hundred and ten billion in this state), and most of that is sent East since the forests of the Central West have been denuded, with the South rapidly following suit. The Sea Food of Puget Sound, Bering Sea and the Pacific is eaten everywhere. The discovery of gold in the Klondike, the consequent opening of Alaska, that "Great Treasure-House of this Nation"; the acquisition of Hawaii and the Philippines, the wars of Japan with China and Russia that have pushed the hands of the Clock of Time ahead a hundred years as to Pacific Ocean developments, warrant the statement that ten and twenty-story buildings here are a wise investment now.

We find only five important exceptions to the HIGH BLUFFS THAT BOUND PUGET SOUND ON THE EAST, namely, at Olympia, Tacoma, Seattle, Everett and Bellingham. Olympia is handicapped by high hills surrounding small tide flats, and by having a tortuous, narrow channel in its first twenty miles toward the ocean. Bellingham is eliminated from the contest for supremacy because of its longer rail haul from Chicago or St. Louis, the center of the United States, with about the same water haul to the ocean that Everett has, though less than from Seattle by twenty miles and Tacoma by about forty-five.

At this point I remind you that the average cost of transportation, per mile by rail is more than ten (sometimes thirty) times as great as by water; and through rail freight seeks the first good harbor. Overland freight from Tacoma to New York is from $28 to $52 a ton. Around the Horn to New York, five times the distance, it is from $5 to $10 a ton. Wheat is hauled from Tacoma to Liverpool at sixteen shillings and six pence a ton. The effect of this difference in cost may be seen in the empty houses and vanished hopes of Port Townsend, Port Angeles and Anacortes, west and northwest of Tacoma. If a convulsion of nature should continue Puget Sound, with a broad deep channel, to Walla Walla, 300 miles east of Tacoma, that would become the great city of the Coast, and the present cities on the Sound would stagnate and deteriorate. THE POINT OF LEAST RESISTANCE IS THE WINNING POINT, always, in Ancient and Modern History.

The folly of hauling twenty freight cars with two engines between Spokane and Everett or Seattle, over the Cascade Mountains by G. N. and N. P. Ry.'s, over three per cent. grades, is soon to cease, and one engine will haul 100 cars via the Columbia & Puget Sound Line, now being built by both roads into THIS, THE FIRST DEPENDABLE HARBOR, on a grade of one-tenth of one per cent., all sloping to the westward. Five times the freight, half the expense, same time. Of course they will not haul this Alaska and Foreign freight by rail farther north to Seattle, forty-two miles, or Everett, seventy miles, because such

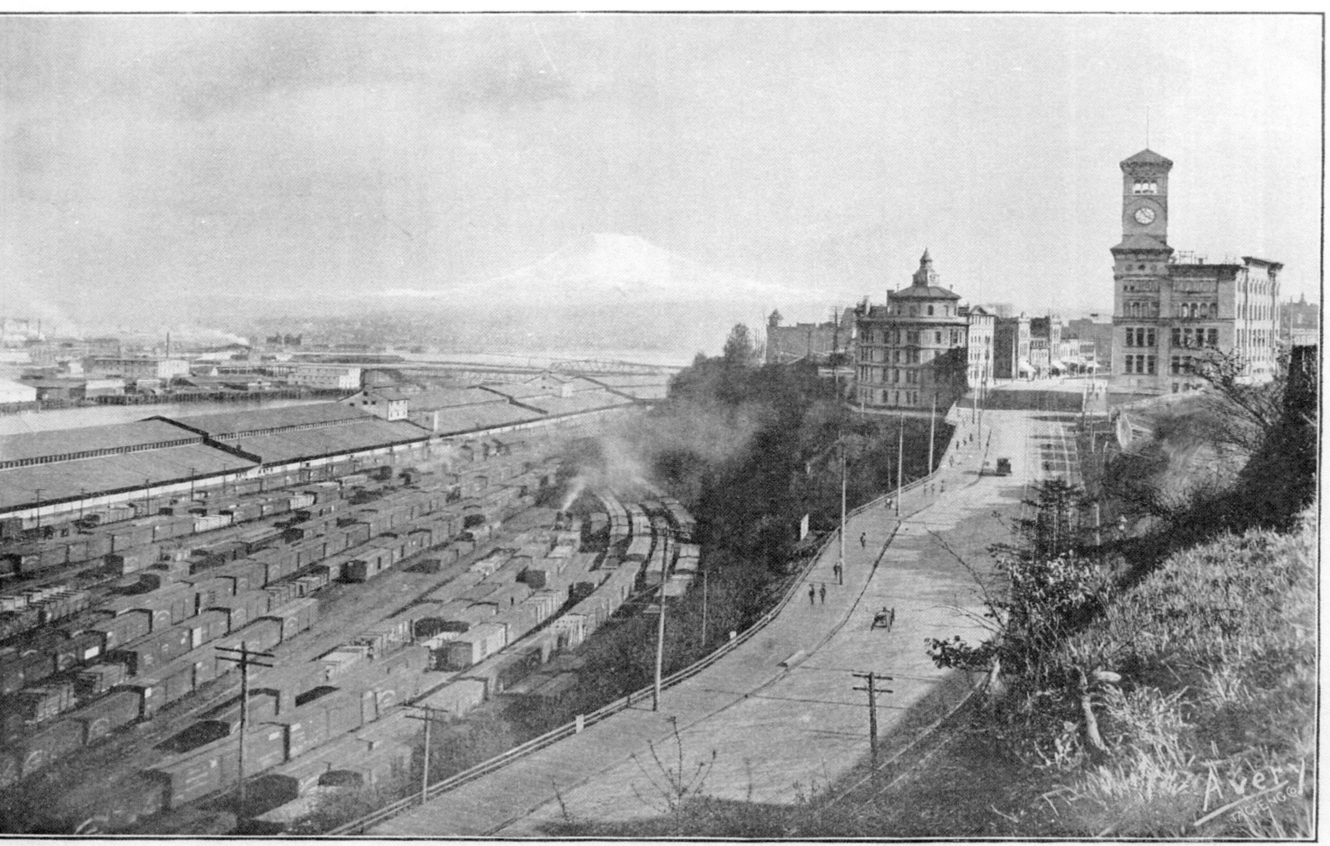

Avery.

GATEWAY OF TACOMA.

Showing Northern Pacific Freight Yards, Wheat Warehouses and Manufacturing District on the Tideflats at Tacoma—Mount Tacoma in the Distance.

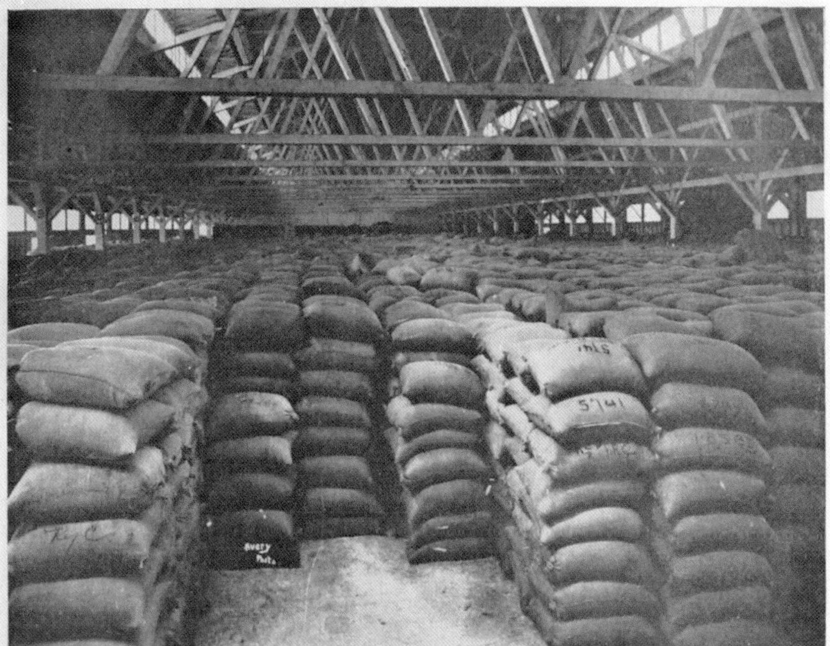

Avery. SECTION OF ONE OF TACOMA'S FAMOUS WHEAT WAREHOUSES.

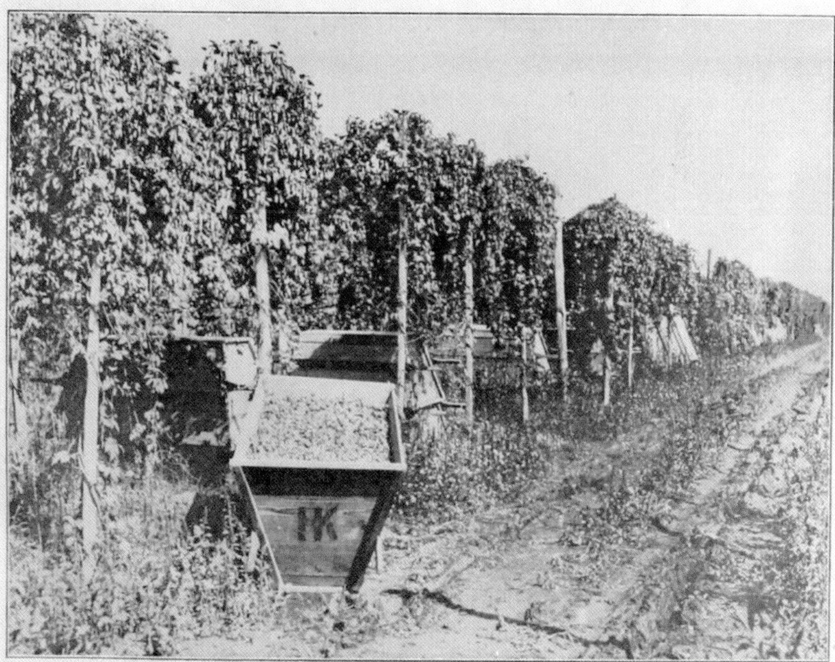

Avery. HOP FIELD IN ONE OF THE MANY PRODUCTIVE VALLEYS TRIBUTARY TO TACOMA.

rail haul will cost as much as 400 miles by water in the case of Seattle, and 700 miles in the case of Everett, above the cost from Tacoma, which is only twenty-five miles by water farther to and from the open Pacific than Seattle, and forty miles farther than Everett. TO TAKE ALASKA AND FOREIGN FREIGHT PAST TACOMA BY RAIL WOULD BE A SILLY FOLLY!

Thus Tacoma THE shipping point, added to THE manufacturing point, will become THE jobbing point; and TACOMA, PREDESTINED BY NATURE BECAUSE IT GAVE NO REAL RIVAL, shall become the city of all three.

Tacoma is twenty years younger than Seattle. Tacoma has been held in check by absence of competing railroads, and by the Indian Reservation on the near east of its water front, 18,000 acres in all, which only lately has been sold for the Indians by a U. S. Government Commissioner to white people, largely far-sighted men of local patriotism. It is fair to ask: "IF SEATTLE HAD SIMILAR DRAWBACKS AND TACOMA FREE FROM THEM, WHAT WOULD BE THEIR RESPECTIVE POPULATION AND PROSPERITY NOW?

In Seattle Post-Intelligencer, Dec. 21, 1902, page six, column three, President Harris, of the Burlington, in an interview said: "A railroad "company must have "ground to do its busi- "ness on, or else turn its "business away. This lat- "ter no city can afford. "Let me show you. In "St. Louis there are up- "wards of 1,300 acres of "lands devoted to the "railroad companies' "uses. This is not too "much, and yet Seattle "would not like me to say "that it can never hope "to get so much business "as St. Louis."

All the level lands in Seattle, filled or to be filled, at Smith's Cove and South Seattle in the Duwamish valley as far south as Georgetown, aggregate less than four thousand acres, and will cost largely over $20,000,000 to fill them. It will be enormously expensive for the railroads to buy or condemn over 1,000 acres of the tide-lands more than they now own, so as to work the traffic for a city the size of the present city of St. Louis. There will be little relief if the Government should build a canal into Lakes Union and Washington, east of Seattle, and open them to navigation, for high bluffs close to the water almost surround both. From Georgetown to Kent, nearly half-way from Seattle to Tacoma, is a long, narrow valley with about 6,000 acres suitable for manufacturing, but more expensive to utilize, owing to switching charges, than if in a compact body. The expense of leveling the high hills that surround Seattle is prohibitive for many years, if not centuries, BUT WOULD BE DONE, IF TACOMA'S GEOGRAPHY AND TOPOGRAPHY DID NOT EXIST.

Nature has done MORE FOR TACOMA THAN FOR BELLINGHAM, EVERETT, SEATTLE AND OLYMPIA COMBINED. The tide-flats and level ground in the valley of the Tacoma river, sometimes called the Puyallup, that can at small cost be channeled for shipping (small cost owing to the gradual slope of the tide-lands to the outer-harbor line instead of rapid as at Seattle) are over two and one-half miles wide, by more than eight miles long. With seven channels therein, as approved by the Government Engineer in charge of the harbor, they will make straight earth pier lines of over seventy (70) miles that, with slips and berths in each of the eight piers, would give more dock mileage than is now in use in New York City, Jersey City and Philadelphia combined.

In the Bay, near the outer harbor line, is a dumping place for the surplus dirt of channel work, consisting of many hundred acres, four hundred feet deep.

The Tacoma Harbor is safer and calmer in stormy weather than is any other large harbor in the world, and it has no superior for anchorage.

In the broad valleys of the Stuck and Puyallup rivers, adjacent to Tacoma, are 20,000 acres of level ground near tide level, other than the 10,000 acres of harbor land that will be channeled. Besides these, there is an accessible plateau of over 130,000 acres of land on the south, as level as Long Island, N. Y. All these two hundred square miles, in addition to portions of the 10,000 acres of harbor lands, and the 20,000 acres of valley lands, are suitable for manufacturing plants with rail tracks to them.

The sloping hillsides of the harbor and valleys of the Greater Tacoma are ideal for home sites, and the level portions are ample for the jobbing and retail trade of a very large city.

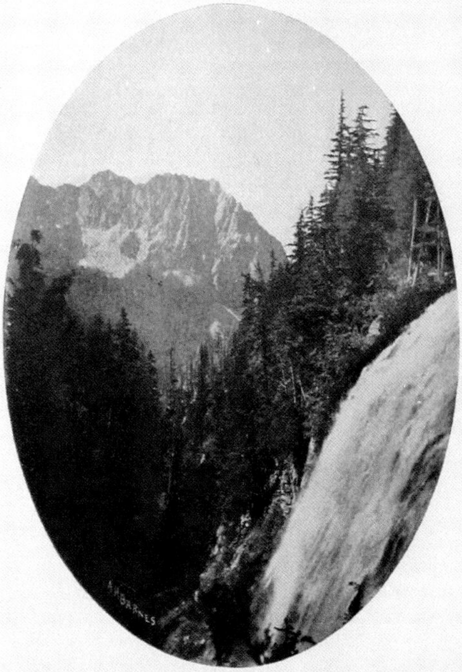

CANYON VIEW OF NARADA FALLS, A DROP OF MORE THAN 175 FEET. EAGLE CLIFF BEND.

Secretary Seward said: "The theatre of the great "events of the future is "the Pacific Ocean." The Paris Figaro recently said, "Contemplate the "wonderful line of the "Asiatic Pacific Coast "from Singapore to Vlad- "ivostock, with the vast "countries of Siberia, "China and Australia. "Contemplate the paral- "lel line of American Pa- "cific Coast from Alaska "to Patagonia, with the "vast countries of Can- "ada, United States and "South America. Sup- "pose there are only two billions on each side, four billions "in all, WILL THE PACIFIC NOT BE, PERFORCE, THE "LAKE OF CIVILIZATION, THE NEW MEDITERRANE- "AN? In truth, the center of the globe's gravity is dis- "placed. And what becomes of Europe, properly speaking, "in this gigantic planetary revolution? It is overwhelmed. "Europe is going to founder. Take America as a whole. Its "fundamental characteristic is still little recognized; small "rainfall in the Old World, abundant in the new; conse- "quently the greatest system of rivers in the latter, and "the only great deserts in the former. THERE IS AS "MUCH ARABLE LAND IN AMERICA AS THERE IS IN "EUROPE, ASIA AND AFRICA COMBINED."

No part of America is more blessed by grand watersheds than the North Pacific Coast, and no city gets greater benefit from them than Tacoma.

This State of Washington, with the beauty of Switzerland and the fertility of ancient Egypt, with its vast and varied resources, with its rich irrigable eastern half and its western half enjoying a semi-tropical climate, owing to the Japan current, will, when the world's population becomes adjusted, support twenty times its present population in comfort; and, if it had thirty times its present population, it would be more self-sustaining than the original thirteen American States are now. This will be conceded when the life-supporting resources of, and external items that contribute to, the respective districts are weighed and balanced.

San Diego and San Pedro are limited by lack of rain fall and of coal. Portland is eliminated as a shipping point, except for small craft, because at the mouth of the Columbia there is a permanent menace, owing to the hard granitic deposit and quick-sand forming a bar, which no system of jetties can remove (the Eads jetties at the mouth of the Mississippi are not parallel, for there a very soft silt is scoured out to deep water). San Francisco is handicapped by up-hill grades aggregating five miles from Chicago, while those of the Northern Pacific to Tacoma are less than three miles, and is further handicapped by the fact that steam vessels leaving San Francisco use Tacoma coal, costing three dollars more per ton for freight from here to that city; and then, they have over 400 miles further to sail to Hongkong than from Tacoma, in an air line 1,140 miles by way of Hawaii; and 700 miles farther from Alaska. It is fair to think that Tacoma, far outside the earthquake belt, WILL ECLIPSE CALIFORNIA PORTS WITHIN A FEW YEARS AS TO OCEAN TRAFFIC in this age of close and closer competition in transportation.

There are no breaks of consequence and therefore no town and harbor sites in the high bluffs along the whole west coast of the United States, other than San Diego Bay, San Pedro, San Francisco Bay, the Columbia River and Puget Sound.

When we look here for cities to correspond to those of the Atlantic Coast, we find San Diego corresponding to Savannah ; San Pedro to Charleston; San Francisco to Baltimore; Portland, Ore., to Newport News and Wilmington. On the north coast of the Pacific, along Puget Sound, we find Bellingham corresponding to Portland, Me.; Everett and Seattle to Providence and Boston, while THE COUNTERPART OF NEW YORK, JERSEY CITY AND PHILADELPHIA CAN BE HAD, AND CAN ONLY BE HAD, IN AND AROUND TACOMA.

Returning to the test of lands and water fronts available for railroading and shipping, we find that Tacoma has over five times as much as Seattle, and Everett less than Seattle. As to level lands for manufacturing and railway trackage other than harbor lands, those adjacent to Tacoma are over twenty-five times as great as those near Seattle, while Everett has more such lands than Seattle and less than one-fifteenth of those of Tacoma.

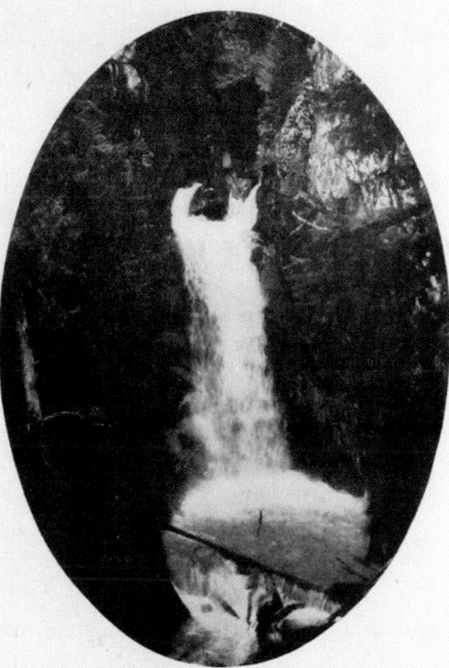

CHRISTINE FALLS, ON VAN TRUMP CREEK, TAKEN FROM A POINT ON THE GOVERNMENT ROAD.

(See Topographic Sheets U. S. Geological Survey, 1894. Tacoma Sheet and Seattle Sheet each ten cents at book stores; or address U. S. Geological Survey Office, Washington, D. C.)

You remember that factories left St. Louis for Chicago because it was found that in Chicago labor performed twenty per cent. more in a year than in the blistering heat of St. Louis, which left men debilitated. Owing to the rich soil of this State and invigorating equable climate throughout the year, I believe manufacturers will find that employees will perform twenty-five per cent. a year more labor here than in the severe extremes of Chicago or New York climates, and in this fruitful land and amiable atmosphere live more cheaply and contentedly than elsewhere. THERE IS MUCH MORE ELECTRIC WATER POWER TO BE DEVELOPED NEAR TACOMA THAN NIAGARA FALLS CAN PRODUCE. This part of the Nation, the center of the raw materials of the world, with water transportation to and from the great cities of the world, should become a great distributor of manufactured goods.

There are great Iron Ore Ranges on this Coast less than 100 miles from tide water harbors. There are thousands of acres of good coking coal lands near Tacoma with downhill haul to the city.

In point of STRATEGICAL IMPORTANCE Tacoma leads all on this Coast, not only because of its coal and its proximity to Alaska and the Orient, but also because the Milwaukee & St. Paul, Wisconsin Central, Soo Line, Burlington, Northwestern, Missouri Pacific, Union Pacific, Santa Fe and Rock Island railways are now eastward in latitudes south of Tacoma; and in coming by as low passes as any now used to the Sound to obtain coal and a short haul to the Orient and Alaska, and to develop their respective territories, fabulously rich, now in the raw, they will, as well as the Northern Pacific, load and unload in Tacoma or lose money every trip by going elsewhere, and the stockholders would soon stop that.

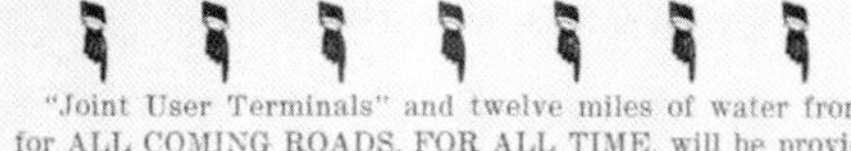

"Joint User Terminals" and twelve miles of water front for ALL COMING ROADS, FOR ALL TIME, will be provided in the Tacoma valley, if plans now started are not stopped, or neglected until too late.

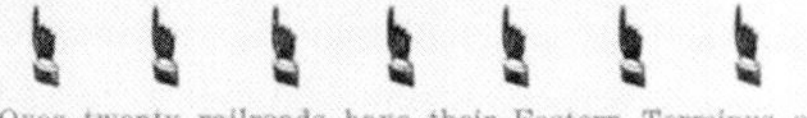

Over twenty railroads have their Eastern Terminus on the Atlantic Coast. The Pacific Coast in time should have forty.

Seattle, Everett, Bellingham and Olympia will all continue to be cities, but hide-bound. Every acre of level land on the east side of Puget Sound will be valuable because there are so few; but those four cit-

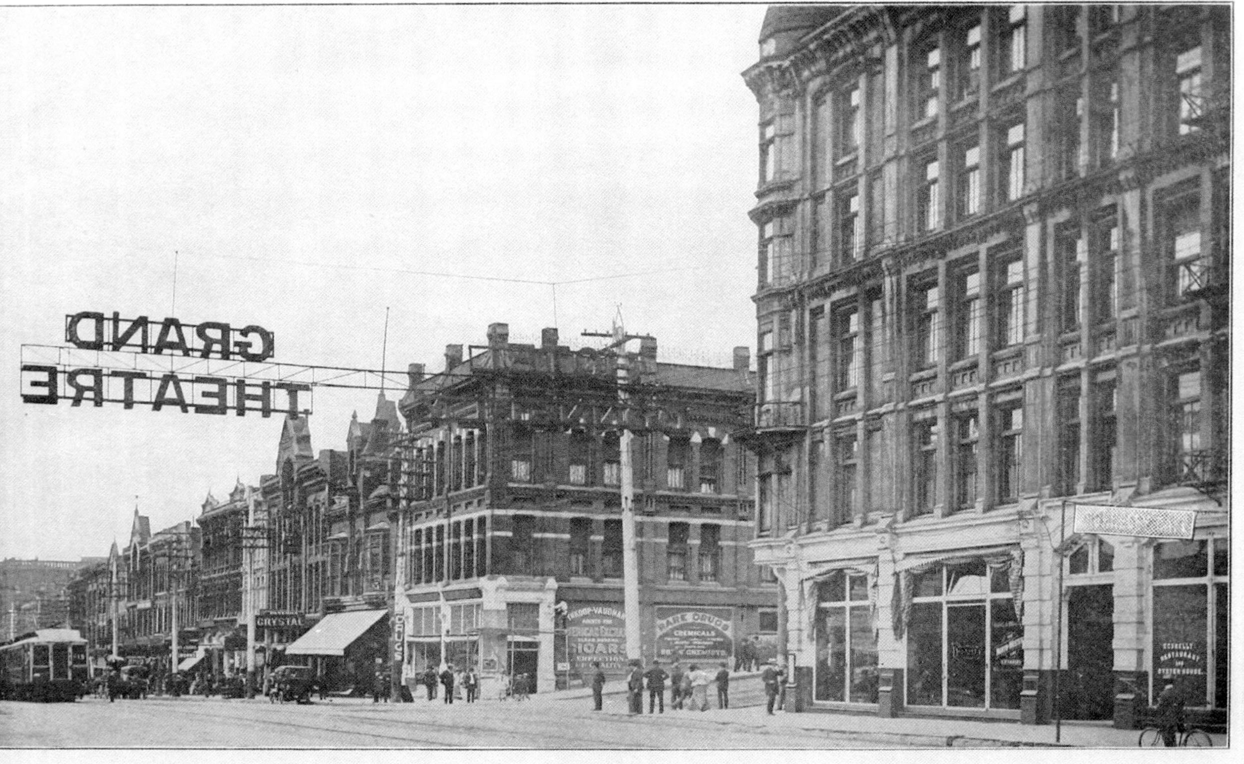

Avery.

PACIFIC AVENUE, FROM NINTH TO ELEVENTH STREET.

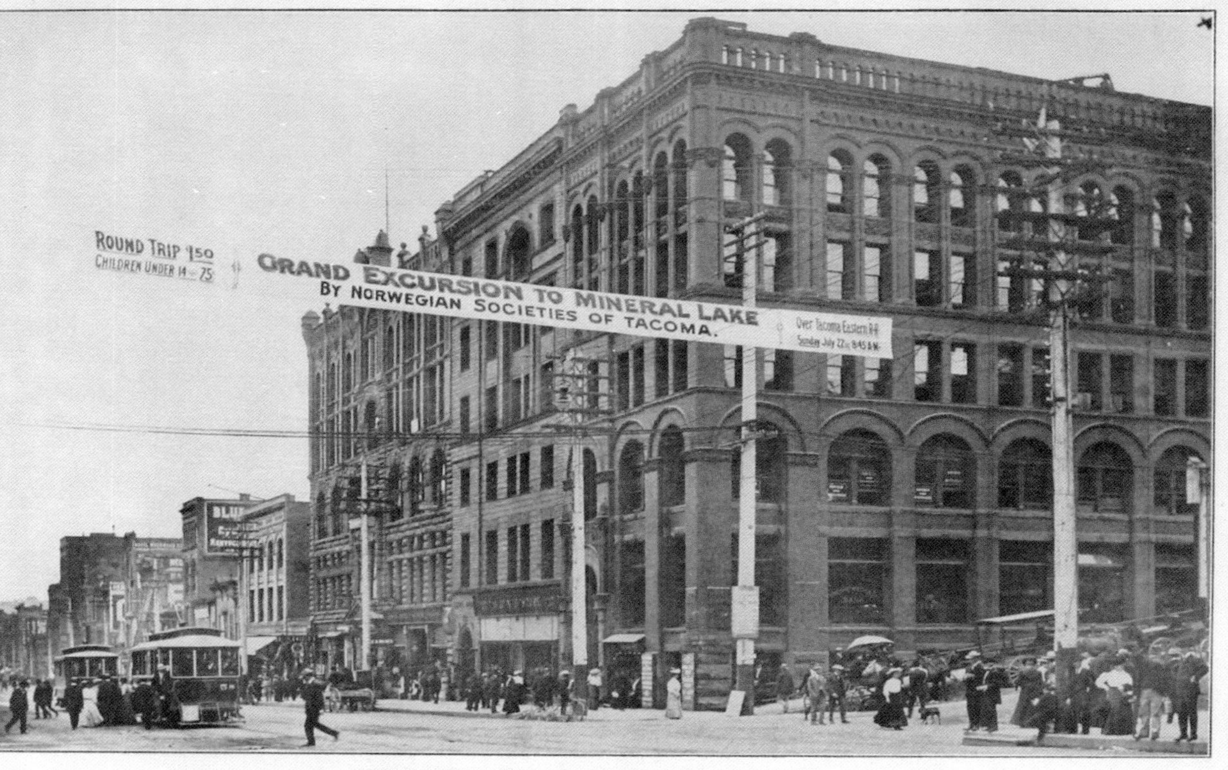

Avery.

PACIFIC AVENUE, FROM ELEVENTH TO THIRTEENTH STREET.

ies are limited and "bottled up" by Nature's high hills.

For the foregoing REASONS, inspired by the example of Chicago with its motto "I Will," Tacoma will become the foremost city of the Coast. Why not of this country and of the world? "When?" Answer: Ultimately! "How soon?" you ask. THAT ALL DEPENDS UPON THE CHARACTERISTICS OF THE PEOPLE.

There is the greatest opening on earth for live men, with their chins up, right here in Tacoma. We need MEN more than money. The bright and brainy men who are here now will welcome the Newcomer of that kind. "Plenty of room at the top"—and all the way up.

Yours truly,

Tacoma, Nov. 1, 1906. DONALD FLETCHER.

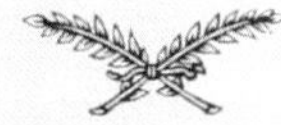

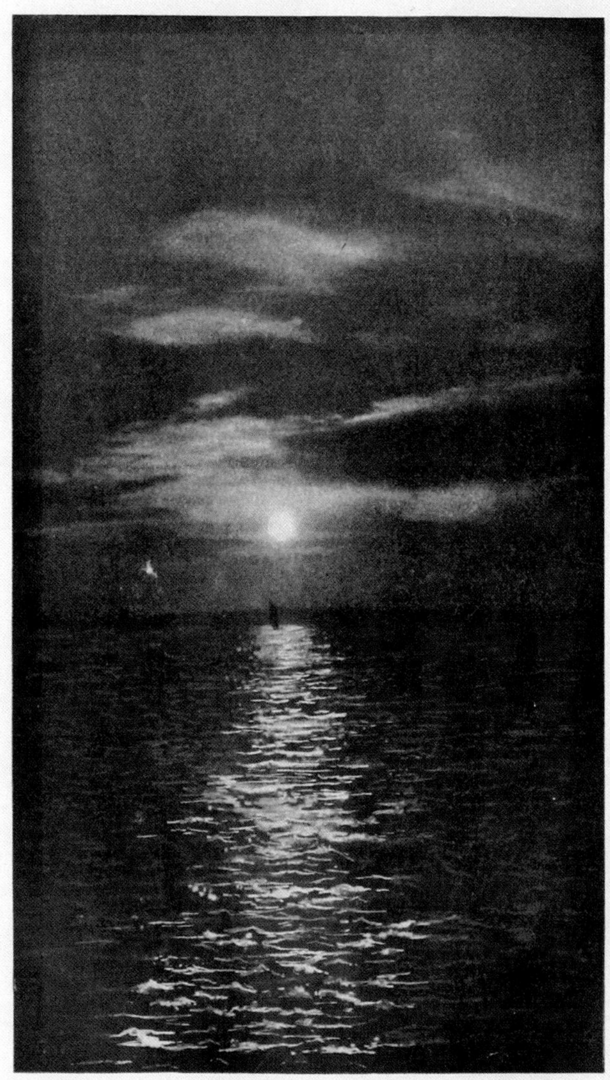

Wonderland, 1906. **EVENING ON PUGET SOUND.**

TACOMA AS GREAT INDUSTRIAL CENTER

Magnificent Harbor, Glorious Climate, Inexhaustible Natural Resources, and Ample Water and Rail Transportation.

By L. W. PRATT, Secretary Tacoma Chamber of Commerce.

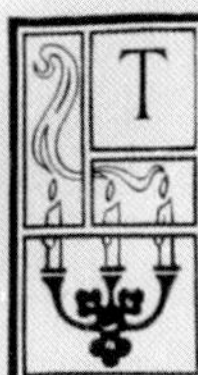

THE year 1906 has been one of extraordinary industrial activity and expansion at Tacoma. The city is exceedingly well favored as a manufacturing point. Its extensive and varied industries are suited to local conditions, both as to production and markets. Location is a most important factor in determining the success of any enterprise, and this is particularly true as to manufacturing. Proximity or access to markets, command of raw materials, transportation facilities, fuel, power, labor conditions, water supply, taxes and the benefits resulting therefrom, and climate have an influence, favorable or unfavorable as the case may be, in determining the fate of an industrial enterprise in any given location. The industries thus far established at Tacoma have generally prospered because the conditions that obtain here are favorable to the particular lines of industrial enterprise that have been undertaken.

Tacoma's access to markets for her products in almost all quarters of the globe is direct. Few manufacturing centers are as favorably located in this respect. As Tacoma is both a rail and ocean terminal point, freight rates are governed by the cheap cost of water transportation to and from points on the Atlantic seaboard or elsewhere where there is actual or possible competition between the two modes of transportation. Established steamship lines operate from Puget Sound to Alaska, San Francisco, Honolulu and New York, Japan, Asiatic Russia, China, Manila, Singapore, and on to Liverpool and Glasgow by the Suez Canal and Metiterranean route, and to Hamburg, Havre, Dunkirk and Marseilles by way of Mexican, Central and South American ports. Hundreds of tramp steamers and sailing vessels are chartered each year to carry Tacoma products to the various ports of the world. In short, in the markets of the Pacific Coast, the Orient and Alaska, the Tacoma manufacturer has a distinct advantage over manufacturers in the same line at any interior or eastern point in the United States. The consumption of American products in these markets is increasing annually at an extraordinary rate. The demand for products which can be economically manufactured at Tacoma may therefore be expected to increase in proportion to the growth of population on the Pacific slope and in Alaska and in pace with our success in the promising and incalculably large markets of the Orient, the Philippines, Hawaii and the Latin republics to the south of us.

There are certain natural avenues of industrial enterprise which are open to Tacoma and in which permanent success is almost absolutely assured. These are the lines of manufacture which utilize the raw materials which can be readily assembled at this city. Tacoma has at command raw materials varied in character and almost unlimited in quantity, including products of agriculture, the forests, mines and fisheries. Few manufacturing centers in the world can show an equal diversity of natural resources. Almost all the products of American agriculture, with the exception of cotton, tobacco and Indian corn, are raised in the country directly tributary to Tacoma, while raw cotton and unmanufactured tobacco are shipped in large quantities through this port to foreign markets. In the manufacture of flour and cereals Tacoma already leads all other points in the United States, west of Minneapolis and Kansas City.

The forests of Western Washington and Oregon supply the material for the great lumber industry of the Northwest, the magnitude of which surpasses anything previously known to the lumber trade, while Tacoma has become the leading point for the manufacture of lumber and products of wood working establishments in the entire United States.

The development of the mineral resources of the Far West has only begun, but Tacoma has already become the headquarters of the smelting industry of the coast and a very important point in the production of lead and copper. The conditions which have favored the reduction of ores at this point will equally affect the development of the iron and steel industry in the near future.

The fisheries of the Pacific are yet in their infancy, but Tacoma enjoys the distinction of having the largest fisheries plant in the United States and ships hundreds of cars of fresh, frozen, cured, salted and pickled fish each year to eastern markets.

No resume of Tacoma's facilities for manufacturing would be complete without special reference to the question of fuel and power. Pittsburg has become the industrial center of the world by reason of the supplies of coking coal in the immediate vicinity. The only coking coal thus far discovered on the Pacific Coast is in Pierce County, and 350 ovens are now in operation within twenty-five miles of Tacoma. This is used extensively in manufacturing in Tacoma, particularly at the smelter, and Pierce County coke will unquestionably be the controlling factor in determining the location at or near Tacoma of the initial plant in the iron and steel industry on the Pacific Coast in the near future.

Cheap electric power is everywhere recognized as a most important factor in industrial development. One naturally thinks of a great waterfall, such as is found at Niagara or Minneapolis, as a natural source of electrical energy, but few recognize until it is pointed out the value of a snow-capped mountain as a power producer. Mount Tacoma, the loftiest mountain peak in the contiguous territory of the United States, is a greater source of power than Niagara Falls, and its harnessed glaciers are already producing tens of thousands of horse power for use in industrial operations at Tacoma. From the snow-line at an elevation of 7,000 feet the water must find its level in the Sound only forty miles away. Fifteen primary glaciers feed in summer the streams which carry off the copious rains of the winter months. The utilization of only two of a great many natural water powers found within a short distance of Tacoma has made it possible for manufacturers to obtain electric power at this city at lower prices than can be obtained at any other point in the United States. The harnessing of Mount Tacoma has only begun.

Again, climatic conditions are exceedingly favorable to industrial enterprises at Tacoma. Freedom from extremes both of heat and cold makes it possible for men to work in comfort throughout the year without appreciable loss of time from bad weather, excessive heat or extreme cold. Labor is efficient and though well paid is cheap to the manufacturer. Tacoma is distinctively recognized as an industrial community and its army of wage earners is well housed and prosperous and constitutes a loyal and progressive body of citizens. Up to the present time no serious labor difficulties have occurred at Tacoma. Every manufacturer recognizes the advantage of a location at a

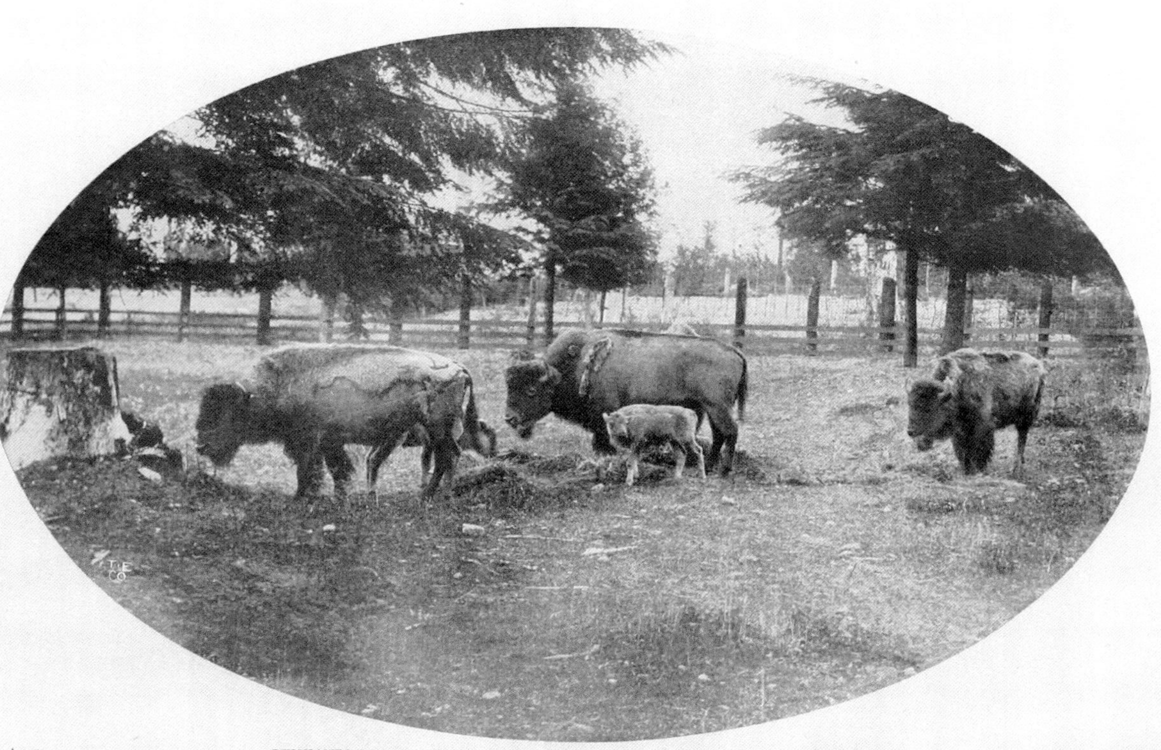

Avery.

REMNANTS OF A DISAPPEARING RACE—BUFFALO AT POINT DEFIANCE PARK.

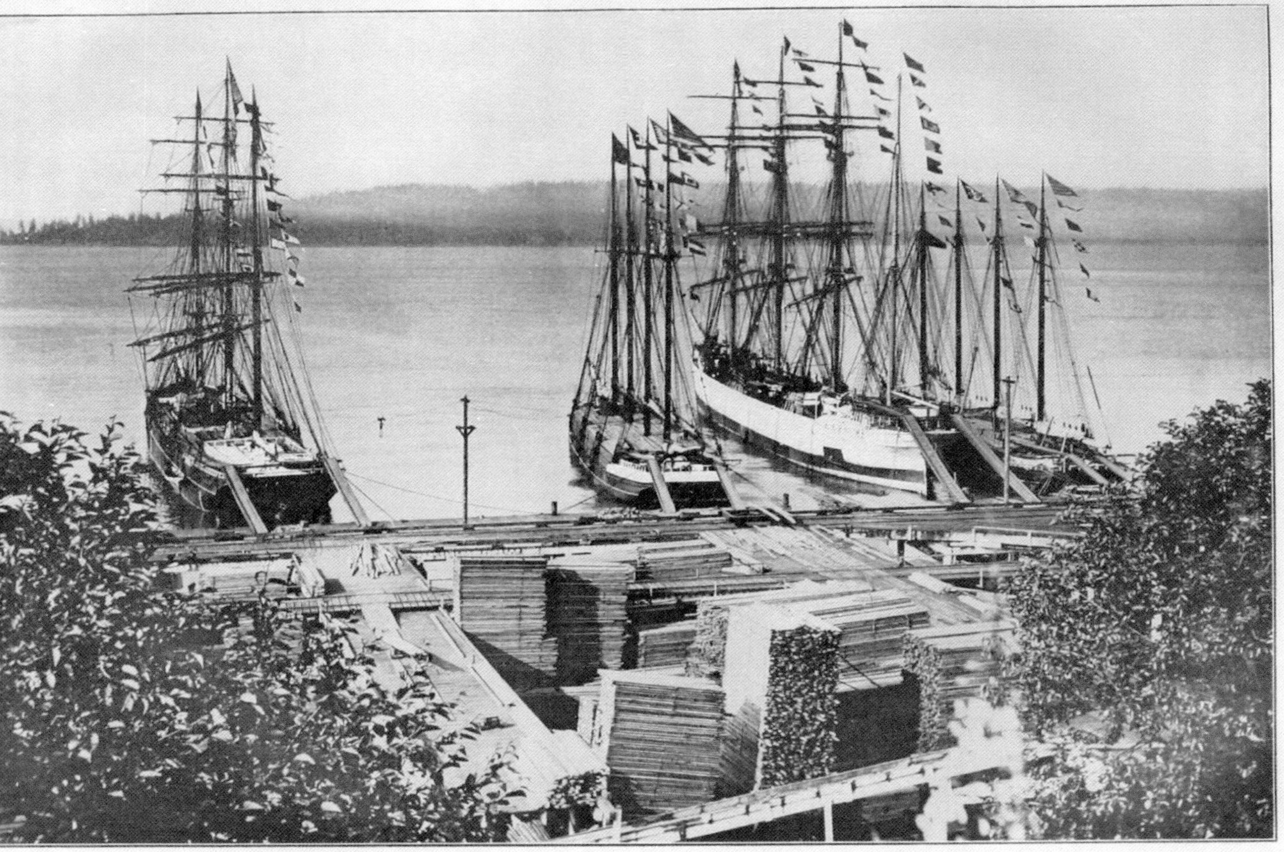

Avery.

LUMBER CARRIERS LOADING AT THE TACOMA MILL COMPANY'S WEARF—FOURTH OF JULY.

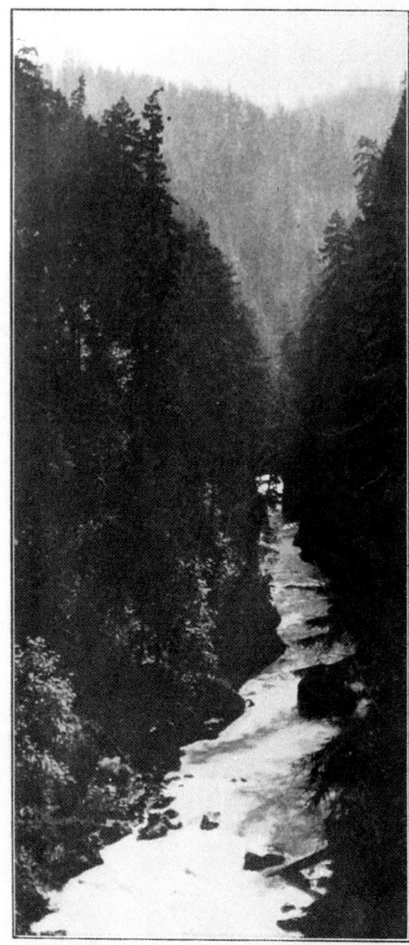

Bedford. NISQUALLY RIVER, LOOKING DOWN CANYON.

good market for labor. The diversity of industries already alluded to is a safeguard against serious results from periods of depression in any one line of industry.

While the question of water supply for a city which is growing as rapidly as Tacoma is generally a serious and perplexing one, and while the details of the solution of the problem for Tacoma have not as yet been fully worked out, there is absolutely no question as to the adequacy and purity of the water that can be obtained. Tacoma is so situated that water can be secured in almost unlimited quantities sufficient to meet the requirements of a great metropolis, at a comparatively low cost. Tacoma is situated at sea level, but the Cascade mountains are only a short distance to the east and the annual rainfall is large enough to insure an abundance of water at all seasons of the year. The greater part of the present supply is obtained from wells on the prairie south of the city, where an unlimited supply of pure and naturally filtered water can be obtained. The cost of pumping can, however, be eliminated by the installation of a gravity system from one of the mountain streams. At the charter election of 1906 a bond issue of $1,680,000 for a gravity supply of 40,000,000 gallons per day from the Green River was authorized by popular vote, and preliminary engineering work is now in progress.

The topography of Tacoma is admirably suited to the requirements of an industrial center. When the harbor improvements on the tide and river flats are completed, more than thirty miles of deep water frontage will be available for commercial and industrial purposes. Manufacturers can obtain sites with both rail and deep water facilities if desired, while thousands of acres of level land in the estuary of the Puyallup river afford ideal sites for manufacturing. For manufacturers who do not require ocean docks and waterfront property the level prairie south of the city is admirably suited. The new railroads which are building into the city from the south or through the Puyallup Valley will add a great many miles of railroad frontage to the sites now available for manufacturing purposes.

The lumber and wood working industries at Tacoma have been very active and prosperous during the year 1906, with only one ground for complaint—namely, the shortage of cars to move the output. Rail shipments of lumber and shingles from Tacoma have, however, broken all previous records during the year. During the twelve months ending with June, 1906, the increase as compared with the previous year was at the rate of 46.4 per cent. Aggravating as the inability to procure cars has been, it must nevertheless be admitted that the actual shipments have increased at a rate far beyond the most sanguine expectations, and little surprise can be expressed at the failure of the railroads to promptly handle the enormous increase in traffic.

The two most important additions to the long list of lumber mills at Tacoma during the year are the new plants of the Dempsey Lumber company and the Defiance Lumber company. The former, on the tide flats on the east side of the Puyallup river, is one of the largest mills in the state and will have a capacity of from 250,000 to 300,000 feet of lumber a day. The work of construction is about complete and the mill will be ready for operation early in 1907. The Defiance Lumber company's new mill on the North End waterfront has a capacity of 100,000 feet a day and the plant is admirably adapted for cargo shipments. Unless unexpected difficulties are encounered in the matter of transportation facilities, or an unlooked for change occurs in conditions throughout the country, the Tacoma lumber cut for the year 1907 may be expected to amount to the unprecedented total of 600,000,000 feet.

One of the most gratifying industrial developments of the year 1906 has been the enlargement of the car and locomotive construction and repair shops of the Northern Pacific Railway at South Tacoma. Fifty-five acres of additional land adjoining the plant on the north were acquired early in the year, a large part of which is already occupied by spurs, rolling stock and construction material, while plans have been prepared for some very large new buildings. The force of men employed at the shops has been greatly increased during the year and the construction of new cars has been carried on on a larger scale than ever before. The enormous demand for cars at this end of the line justifies the belief that the car building industry at Tacoma will continue to expand and will grow to enormous proportions.

Extensive improvements and enlargements have also been made during the past year at the Tacoma smelter, particularly in the copper department. One of the significant changes during the year at the smelter was the voluntary adoption by the management of an 8-hour day with three shifts of men in 24 hours, in place of two. This necessitated a considerable increase in the force. It has been announced that further and very extensive enlargements at this plant are shortly to be made. In the natural development of the copper industry at Tacoma a copper rolling mill and copper wire works are expected to follow the successful establishemnt of the copper refinery, the capacity of which has been largely increased during the past year. Large shipments of copper ingots to Europe have been made during the year by steamers of the Tacoma-Liverpool line, the steamers going directly to the smelter docks for cargo. During the year the smelter has acquired extensive coal deposits at Fairfax and owns and operates a large number of coke ovens at that point.

Another important industrial development during the past year has been the purchase of a site of 3300 acres southwest of the city for an enormous plant to be erected by the Dupont Powder company. The work of construction is now in progress. Tacoma will shortly supply the material of greatest importance in mining operations in Alaska and the Pacific Coast. Next to labor, the cost of explosives is the most expensive factor in mining. The establishment of this plant near Tacoma will enormously increase the volume and value of Tacoma's shipments to Alaska.

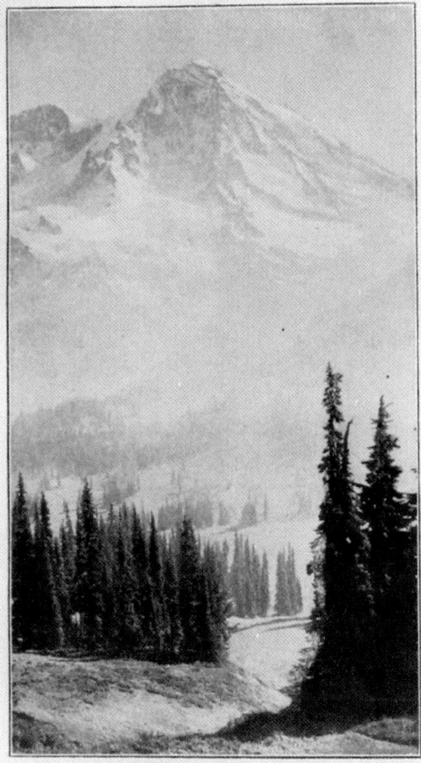

Barnes. MORNING VIEW OF MOUNT TACOMA.

Two important industries which utilize Alaska products have been established at Tacoma during the past year. One of these is the Pacific Coast Gypsum company, whose extensive plant on the east side of the city waterway north of the Eleventh street bridge, began operations in the early summer. Just south of the Eleventh street bridge on the east side of the waterway are the works of the Western Marble company, which have been in operation for several months and are now being greatly enlarged. Four thousand tons of marble from Shakan, Prince of Wales Island, were shipped to this plant during the year, and ten thousand tons will be handled in 1907, and sawed and polished for building purposes.

In the manufacturing industry at the head of the bay, some noticeable improvemetns have been made during the year. One of these is the new four-story brick and concrete plant of the Tacoma Biscuit and Candy company. The Stilson-Kellogg Shoe company's factory has been raised to five stories and a new factory has been erected for the Shull-Day company, manufacturers of overalls. Other noticeable additions to the long line of miscellaneous industries in Tacoma are to be found in the Center street district along the Northern Pacific line to Portland. One of the new buildings in that section is occupied by the Davies Bros. Electrical company for the manufacture of electric lamps and fixtures. The plant of the Northwest Conserving company has been greatly enlarged and improved and doubled in capacity.

On the tide flats, the big plant of the Carstens Pasking company shows several important additions. One of the new buildings has been equipped with machinery from Milwaukee for a wool sheep-skin tannery and a wool pullery, which will shortly be in operation. A large number of other industries have been established during the year which are scattered through the business part of the city. The industrial expansion of the year 1906 undoubtedly exceeds that of any previous year in the history of the city. The growth of industries in the suburbs has also been gratifying. Tacoma capital has been invested in the new works of the Acme Malleable Iron company, which is nearing completion at Meeker Junction, southeast of the city. Along the line of the Tacoma Eastern railroad there has been a large increase in lumber manufacturing, chiefly by concerns which are owned and operated from this city. It is to be expected that a great deal of the industrial development of the future which will center at Tacoma will spread out over the territory within a radius of fifteen or twenty miles from the business center and in a territory exclusively tributary to Tacoma and identified with it in interest, though not actually within the municipal boundaries. The Tacoma smelter, for example, is located just outside of the city limits. The growth of the community at the smelter has been such as to lead to the incorporation during the past year of "Ruston." In the natural course of development other towns will be incorporated in the vicinity of the city, which later on will request annexation and become part of the Greater Tacoma of the future, the Industrial Center of the Pacific Northwest.

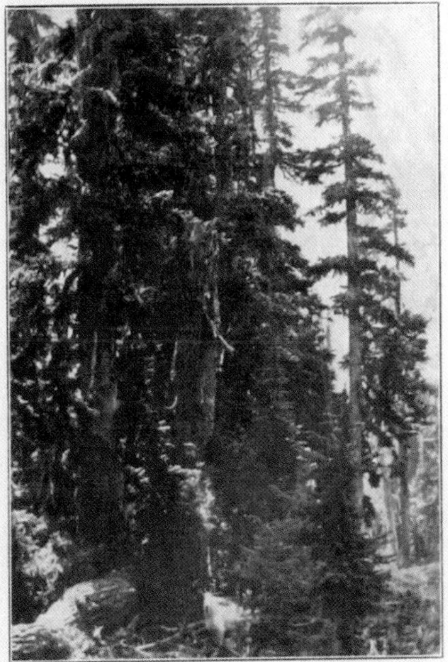

MOUNTAIN GOAT IN INDIAN HENRY'S HUNTING GROUNDS.

Barnes. Seventy feet distant when "shot" by the camera.

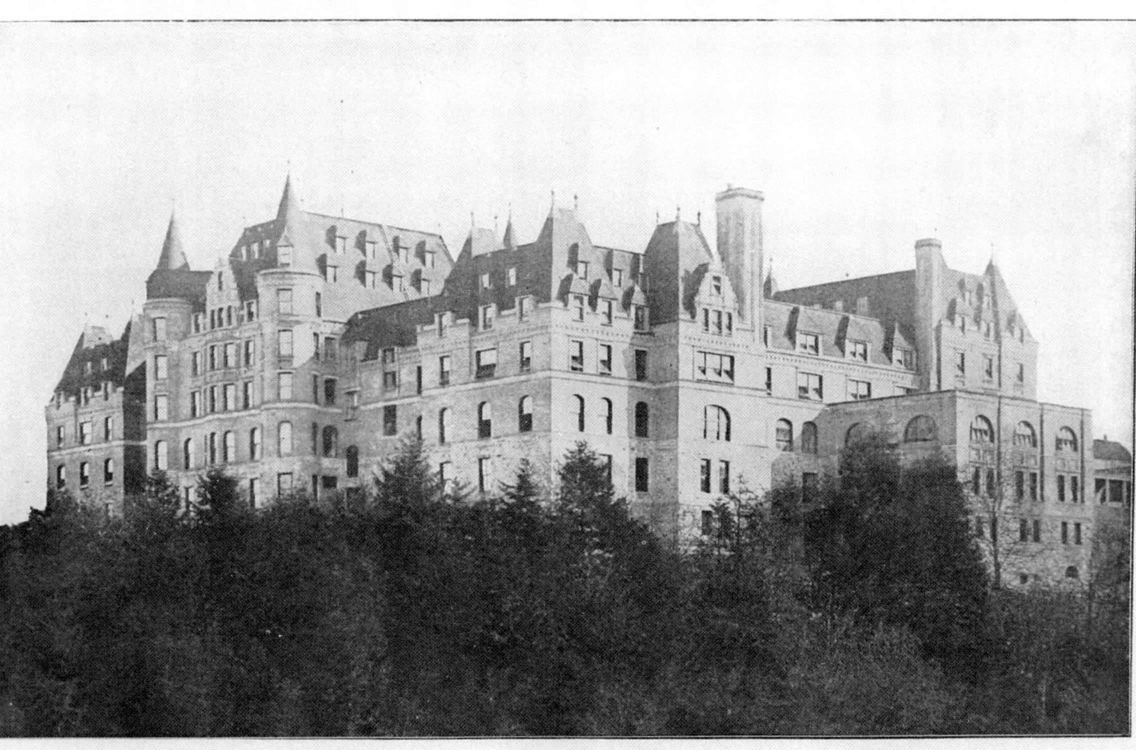

Avery.

A NEW VIEW OF TACOMA'S HIGH SCHOOL.
Completed During 1906 at a Cost of Upward of $500,000.

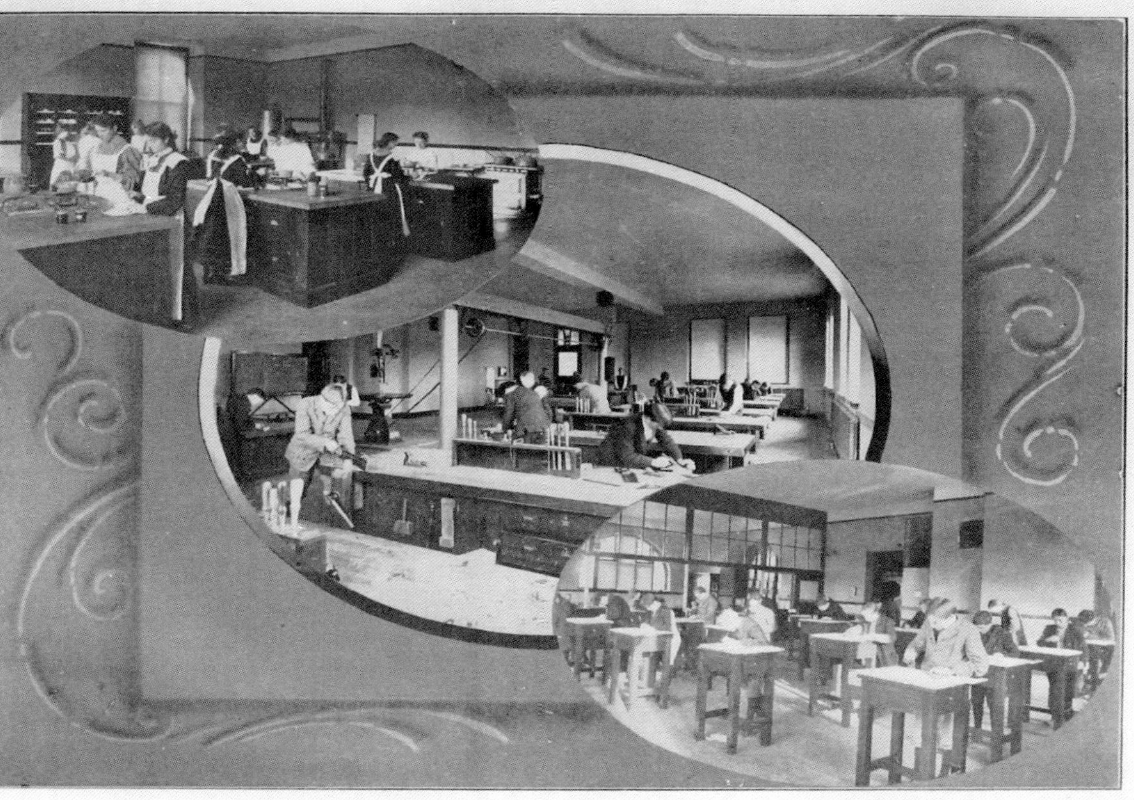

Avery.

MANUAL TRAINING IN THE TACOMA HIGH SCHOOL.

THE FINANCIAL SITUATION

Tacoma Has Successful and Stable Banking Institutions — Clearings Increase 650 per cent. in Ten Years

By P. C. KAUFFMAN, Second Vice President Fidelity Trust Company.

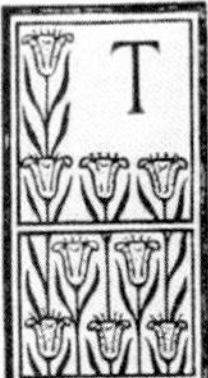

THE year 1906 has been especially marked as the most prosperous in Tacoma's history, and 1907 opens with promise of even greater things. The wonderful increase in the volume of general business is well reflected in the reports of the Clearing House Association and statements of the banks. The various financial institutions in Tacoma report the year 1906 as being the most prosperous in their history, and each one has made a substantial addition to its undivided profit account. Three new banks have been established during the year, and each reports a very satisfactory volume of business. The growth in deposits in the past twelve months has been especially marked, the combined deposits at the close of 1906, in round numbers, being $15,000,000, as against $10,000,000 at the close of 1905, a gain of fully $5,000,000, or 50 per cent. This gain in deposits has been equitably distributed, each of the several banks showing a proportionate increase.

The bank clearings for the year largely exceeded those of any previous year, each month showing a decided gain over the clearings of the corresponding months in 1905, while the total for the year of $204,962,372 shows a gain of $40,007,318 over the clearings of 1905, and $89,168,511 over the clearings of 1904. It is interesting in this connection, in order to obtain a fair idea of Tacoma's commercial and financial expansion, to make a comparison with 1896, when bank deposits, clearings and general business were at the lowest point of depression, resultant upon the panic of 1893. The total clearings for the year 1896 are shown by the records of the Tacoma Clearing House Association to have been but $27,083,966, or $13,506,711 less than the combined clearings of the two months of November and December, 1906. The total clearings for the year 1906 were $204,962,372, which shows a gain over the clearings of 1896 of $177,878,406, or over 650 per cent.

The two following tables will be especially interesting as furnishing an adequate statement of the remarkable expansion of business in Tacoma, the first showing the clearings for the past four years by months:

Tacoma Bank Clearings.

Month—	1903.	1904.	1905.	1906.
January ..	$ 8,969,399	$ 8,719,901	$ 11,829,658	$ 16,045,040
February .	7,521,157	8,175,534	9,857,362	14,751,368
March	8,639,381	9,144,349	12,774,318	17,079,260
April	8,162,921	8,231,910	12,146,767	15,899,099
May	7,965,403	8,299,839	14,241,901	16,476,142
June	7,767,707	8,279,924	13,322,630	15,574,771
July	7,715,580	7,652,588	13,567,574	15,714,512
August ...	7,308,197	8,151,961	13,468,185	16,178,598
Sept'ber ..	8,330,087	9,589,443	14,134,518	16,100,179
October .	9,268,786	12,649,087	15,662,226	20,552,707
Nov'mber	8,764,691	12,968,242	16,579,307	19,494,061
December	10,060,855	13,931,084	17,370,608	21,041,618
Totals ..	$100,474,164	$115,793,861	$164,955,054	$204,962,372

The second table, showing the clearings for each year from 1896 to 1906, inclusive:

1896	$ 27,083,966.44
1897	28,921,480.37
1898	43,126,143.93
1899	45,389,836.18
1900	53,762,587.12
1901	59,622,649.65
1902	75,749,763.38
1903	100,474,164.08
1904	115,793,859.78
1905	164,955,054.32
1906	204,265,737.00

This great increase in banking activity is easily accounted for when the wonderful increase in all lines of trade, business, and commerce is considered. The 400-odd manufacturing concerns of Tacoma, with a capitalization of $11,000,000, employing an army of 15,000 employes, with a monthly pay-roll of $800,000, produced an output during the year valued at over $40,000,000, a very large increase over any preceding year. The jobbing trade of Tacoma increased wonderfully during the year, aggregating close to $38,000,000, an increase of $5,000,000 over 1905. Most of Tacoma's largest wholesale concerns have erected and are now housed in substantial new buildings that will greatly facilitate their rapidly growing trade. The expenditure during the year by the Union Pacific and Chicago, Milwaukee and St. Paul Railway Companies of $8,000,000 in the acquisition of terminal facilities in the city of Tacoma and recognition of the fact that it will require the expenditure of another $8,000,000 to make these terminals available, gave a remarkable impulse to business in all lines, and it seems certain that, owing to its unsurpassed wharf and dockage facilities, Tacoma is destined to become the main entrepot for the great future commerce of the Orient. The rapidity with which this commerce is growing is evidenced by the following table:

Ocean Commerce of the Port of Tacoma.

By fiscal years from 1900 to 1906—	Value.
1900	$22,803,773
1901	29,189,163
1902	39,133,813
1903	36,570,765
1904	37,410,682
1905	46,808,976
1906	50,084,215

The Tacoma banks handled a large part of this vast business, which contributed greatly to the remarkable advance in clearings.

The outlook for the coming year is most encouraging. In fact, it seems assured that the year 1907 will show a gain in all lines of business far surpassing any previous year.

The building record of 1906 exceeded that of any previous year since the founding of the city, many millions of dollars having been expended in the construction of new buildings, while miles of beautifully paved streets were constructed by the city at a further expenditure of millions, and millions more by the street railway companies in extensions and improvement of their lines. During the coming year the street car lines will spend additional millions in further much-needed extensions, and it is assured that Tacoma will have a series of street railway systems unsurpassed by any city of its size in the country.

Both the Sunset Telephone Company and the Independent Telephone Company during the year just closed put under ground all their lines in the business section of the city and the paved portion of the residence section, at a very heavy expenditure, which was largely added to by the installing of the latest and most improved switchboards.

Tacoma claims justly to be the industrial center of the Pacific Northwest, and bases its claims on the following facts: It—

Has the largest wheat warehouse in the world — 2,350 feet long.

Manufactures more lumber and products of wood-working factories than any other city in the world.

Mills more flour than any other city west of Minneapolis and Kansas City.

Reduces more ore than any other city west of the Rocky Mountains.

Has the largest private drydock north of San Francisco.

five years and has well earned its motto, "Watch Tacoma Grow."

Has the largest fisheries plant in the United States.

Population.

1870	73
1880	1,093
1900	37,714
1906	85,000

The growth of the state of Washington is commensurate with that of its large cities, the figures for the year being remarkable. The aggregate value of the agricultural and horticultural crops of the state for the year was close to $100,000,000, so that the banks in the interior cities are fairly overflowing with money.

To illustrate the growth in bank deposits: The total deposits of the banks of the three cities, Seattle, Tacoma and Spokane, were, at the date of the controller's last call, $103,000,000, or two and a half times the entire deposits of

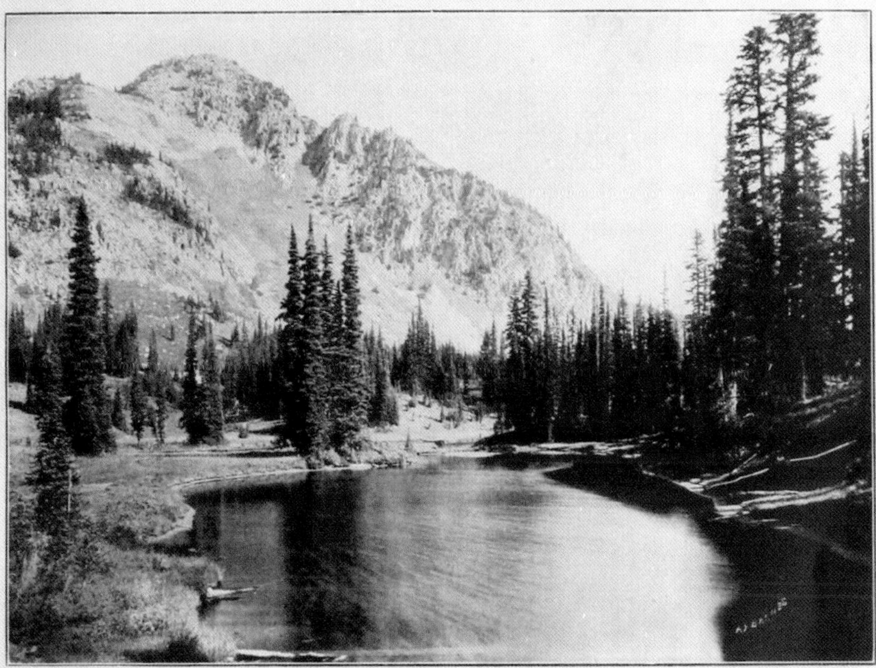

Barnes. LAKE IN INDIAN HENRY'S HUNTING GROUNDS, PARADISE PARK.

Has the largest car and locomotive construction and repair plant in the Pacific Northwest.

Has the largest meat packing industry west of Denver.

Employs more than 15,000 men in manufacturing industries.

Has gained more than two new industries a month for five years.

Tacoma has unlimited supplies of cheap electric power from the harnessed glaciers of Mount Tacoma for manufacturing.

Tacoma has abundance of coal and coke, produced within twenty-five miles, and cheap fuel from the waste of the lumber mills.

Tacoma handles the largest share of the leading natural products of the Pacific Northwest—timber, coal, ores, grain, fish and furs.

Tacoma's population has more than doubled in the past

the state in 1901, just five years ago. A conservative estimate shows that the banks of the state of Washington are today creditors of the East to the extent of fully $30,000,000 in call loans, commercial paper and stocks and bonds purchased and held as liquid assets.

With confidence in the future, Tacoma extends a hearty invitation to all who desire to be in the very center of the world's greatest commercial development to locate within her limits, and to every one that comes eager to do his part in this great undertaking Tacoma will give a most cordial welcome.

Tacoma is noted for her many excellent public and private schools. In the number and character of her private institutions of learning she surpasses any other city in the state. Among these may be mentioned: Whitworth College and University of Puget Sound, for both ladies and gentlemen; Annie Wright Seminary, for ladies, and the Lutheran University at Parkland, a suburb of Tacoma.

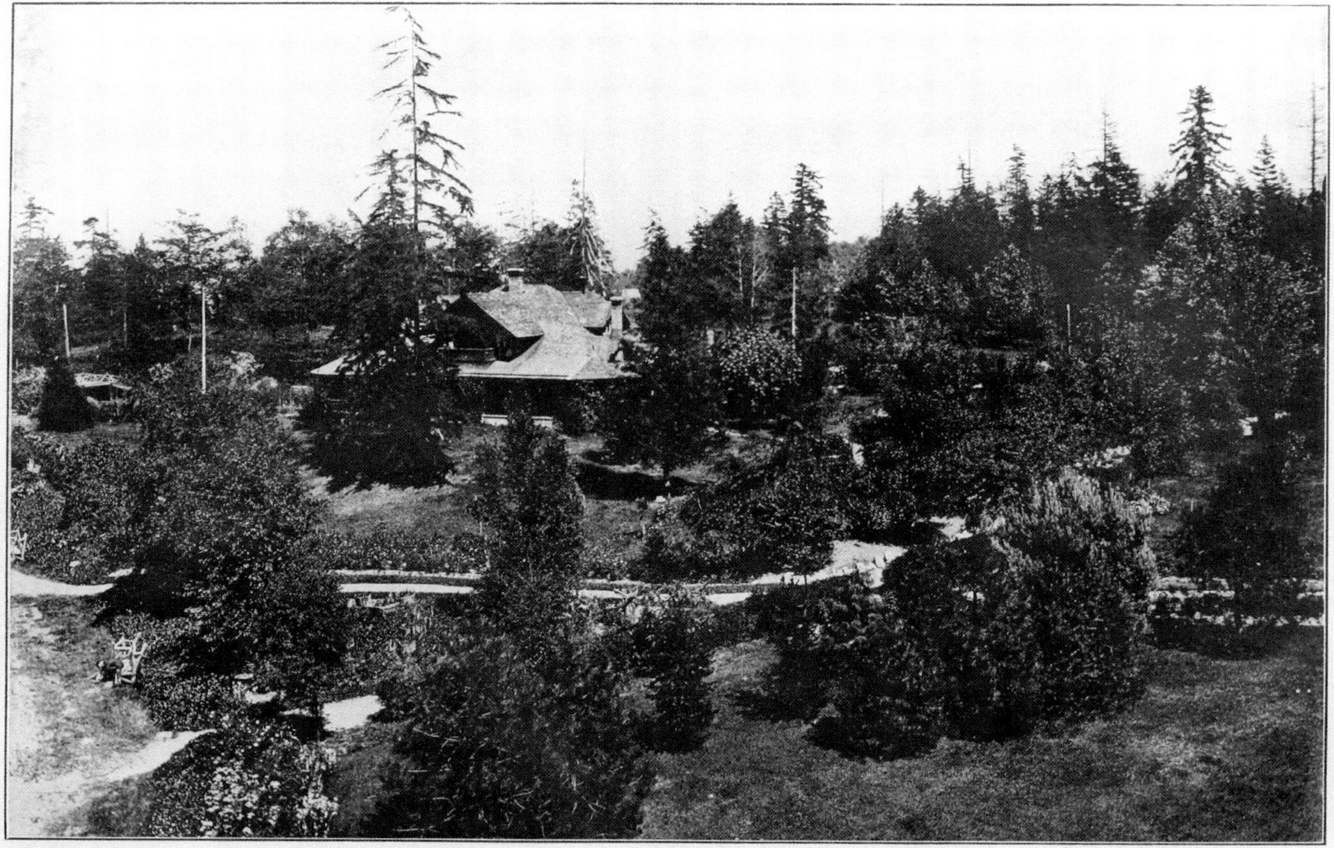

Avery.

IN POINT DEFIANCE PARK—RESIDENCE OF SUPERINTENDENT ROBERTS.

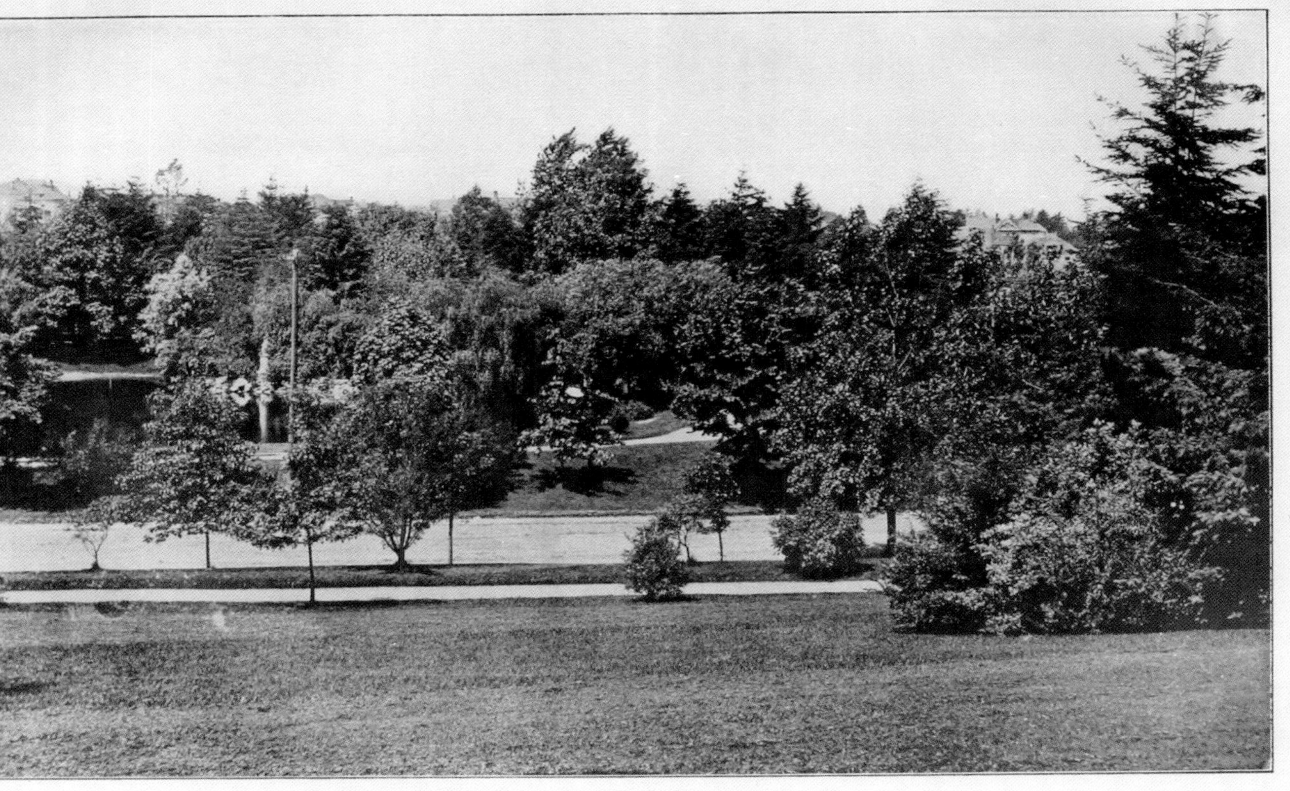

Avery.

SECTION OF WRIGHT PARK, SHOWING THE MINIATURE LAKE.

HISTORICAL SKETCH OF TACOMA

Early Settlement — How City Was Named — Through Boom Days and Panic to Era of Great Prosperity

By C. L. B.

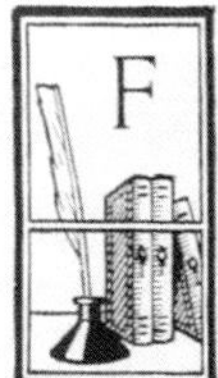

FIRST: A tribute of affection to the man who gave us the name "Tacoma," Theodore Winthrop, the young poet-patriot of a noble race, whose beautiful descriptions of our glorious scenery have endured for half a century as the best, though he only passed, in canoe and saddle, through this region, where duller minds have vegetated a lifetime without painting a picture in either words or colors that gives any adequate idea of the grandeur that surrounds them. This service from the great writer whose book reflected the soul's response to nature's beauty, has met a deserved recognition lately from a local improvement club, which has given the name "Winthrop Heights" to the section of our city overlooking the most beautiful part of the scenery and commanding a view of the point around which Winthrop's canoe floated that misty August day in 1853, when the poet first beheld our mountain, whose name he, and he alone, adapted to its present form from his Indian guides' gutteral and varying "Tachoma, Tahoma, Tak-koma, Tacoma."

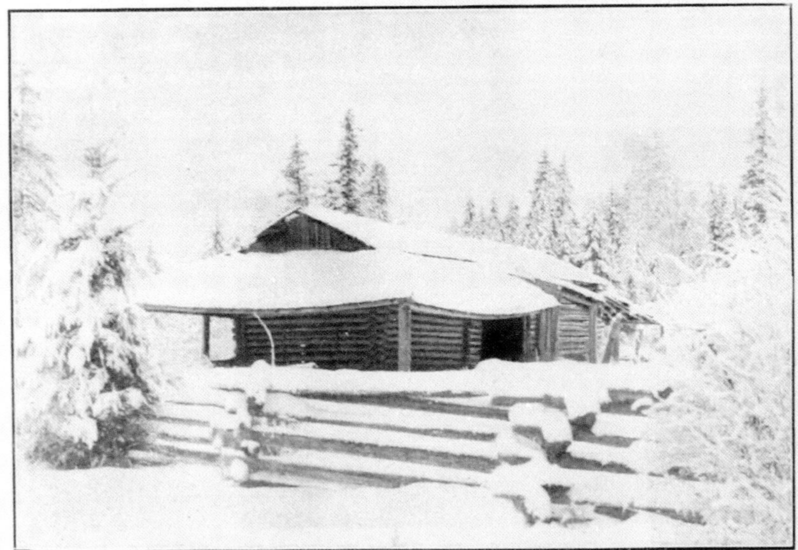

Barnes. A WINTER OF LONG AGO — PIONEER BARN NEAR TACOMA OVER FIFTY YEARS OLD.

As for our city, none can dispute that nature has willed there shall be a city here. None of all the Eastern or Middle states has as many advantages combined to make a great city as we have: The cheapest power for manufacturing in the world; good harbor; good railroad connections; abundant agricultural resources; a plentiful supply of merchantable and fuel woods, of useful and precious minerals and the facilities for smelting and refining them; fine fisheries; healthful climate, mild and equable, unique among the various violent extremes to be found in our country, from the 130 below zero of the North (in exactly our latitude) to the 130 degrees above in torrid regions, while Puget Sound remains placidly between 34 and 80 degrees, its normal temperature in the sixties.

Tacoma stands as a magnificent illustration of the truth of genial Tom Benton's assertion, made more than seventy years ago, in his effort to induce Congress to build a railroad to the Pacific, that the way to India was not across the Atlantic, but across the Pacific; for Tacoma now stands, a gateway to the Orient, where the "rails meet the sails," connecting the Atlantic with the Pacific.

The story of how the railroad finally came has often been told. Tacoma, more than any other city on the Pacific Coast, demonstrated the supreme advantage of being the terminal point on Puget Sound of one of the great transcontinental lines, the Northern Pacific railroad; and now, in the second stage of her development, spite of subsequent discriminations against her by methods whose abuses in general are promised correction by our government, two more lines, the Milwaukee and the Union Pacific, are completing preliminaries for an entrance here.

To understand fully the causes leading up to the foundation of Tacoma and to its selection as a site, it is necessary briefly to review the history of the great railway enterprise which founded our city. Early prophets of a transcontinental railroad, beside the most important, "Missouri compromise" Tom Benton, the first of our prominent men to appreciate the possibilities of the Far West (which he learned from Lewis and Clark, after their return from their journey of discovery), were Rev. Samuel Parker, in 1835; Dr. Samuel Barlow, of Massachusetts, in 1837, and especially Asa Whitney, who by public meetings agitated the building of a road connecting Lake Michigan with the Columbia river. Finally, in 1853, Congress made an appropriation of $150,000 for the survey of railroad routes from the Mississippi river to the Pacific Ocean. Isaac I. Stevens (later Governor Stevens) was intrusted with the survey of the northern route, while a corps of surveyors under orders from the war department began a survey in 1853 from Puget Sound, over the Cascade range, to meet Stevens' force—the same whose work was met by Winthrop in his trip across the mountains on the horse purchased at Nisqually. In 1857 an act to incorporate the Northern Pacific Company was passed by the territorial legislature of Washington, but it was not until 1864 that the charter was formally granted by Congress to the Northern Pacific, the franchise including a grant of lands to aid in the construction of a railroad and telegraph line from Lake Superior to Puget Sound. In 1870 the work was begun; in 1873 the company, at a meeting in New York, formally declared its Western terminus at Tacoma. In September of that year came the great panic, the failure of Jay Cooke resulting in the stoppage of the Northern Pacific operations. The contractors building the line from Kalama to Tacoma were unable to pay their men. It was necessary to reach Tacoma before the end of the year to meet the requirements of the charter. Sixteen miles remained to be completed. The railroad company, through the individual efforts of some of its officers, completed the road into Tacoma the day before the limit prescribed by the charter. In 1877 the first portion of the Cascade branch was built, connecting Tacoma with Wilkeson. In 1881 Villard selected the Stampede pass as the route across the Cascades, and in 1887 the first through train arrived in Tacoma from St. Paul.

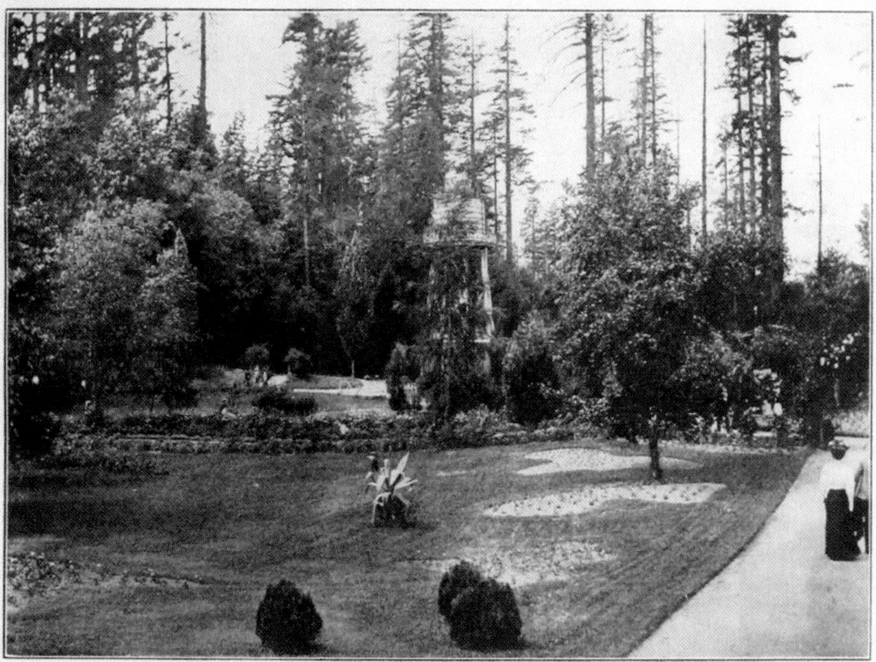

Avery. ENTERING POINT DEFIANCE PARK.

The first white settlement in Tacoma was made by Nicholas De Lin in 1852, the year that old Fort Steilacoom was established. "De Lin's sawmill at the mouth of the Puyallup" was the name. In 1853 his partner, Barnhart, left his claim, which was taken up by Peter Judson, father of Stephen and John Paul Judson. This claim extended from what is now Seventeenth street to the City Hall, and up the hill. In 1855 the Indian war broke out, its inciting cause the white man's coveting the Indians' fertile farm lands. By the trickery of the Medicine Creek (Nisqually) treaty, many tribes lost their lands, and the Nisqually tribe were also notified by Governor Stevens (against whose administration this act will always remain as a blot) that they must by a certain day abandon their productive valley farms and be confined to the salt meadows and thick forests, where neither grass for their horses nor food for themselves could be raised. But Leschi, the Nisqually chief, was a warrior, and he aroused the tribes to resist this injustice. They combined for an uprising, and only the warning of a friendly squaw to the white settlers saved them from a general massacre, giving them time to flee to Fort Steilacoom for refuge the day before the attack took place, when farm buildings were burned, and the White river valley settlers, who had been assured by the acting governor that there was no danger, were slain, men, women and children. Throughout the war Leschi showed himself to be a brave and magnanimous warrior, saving the women and children of his enemies when possible. The hostile Indians were not driven out of the valleys until 1856. Leschi then crossed the mountains and fought with the Yakimas. When peace was made Leschi surrendered to the federal troops, under a guarantee of pardon. But the territorial authorities would not agree to this, and Leschi was betrayed into their hands by a renegade Nisqually for $500. He was tried for "murder," in having taken part in a war where men were killed—a most unheard-of violation of precedent, impossible of imposing on a white man—and Governor Stevens concurred. Judges

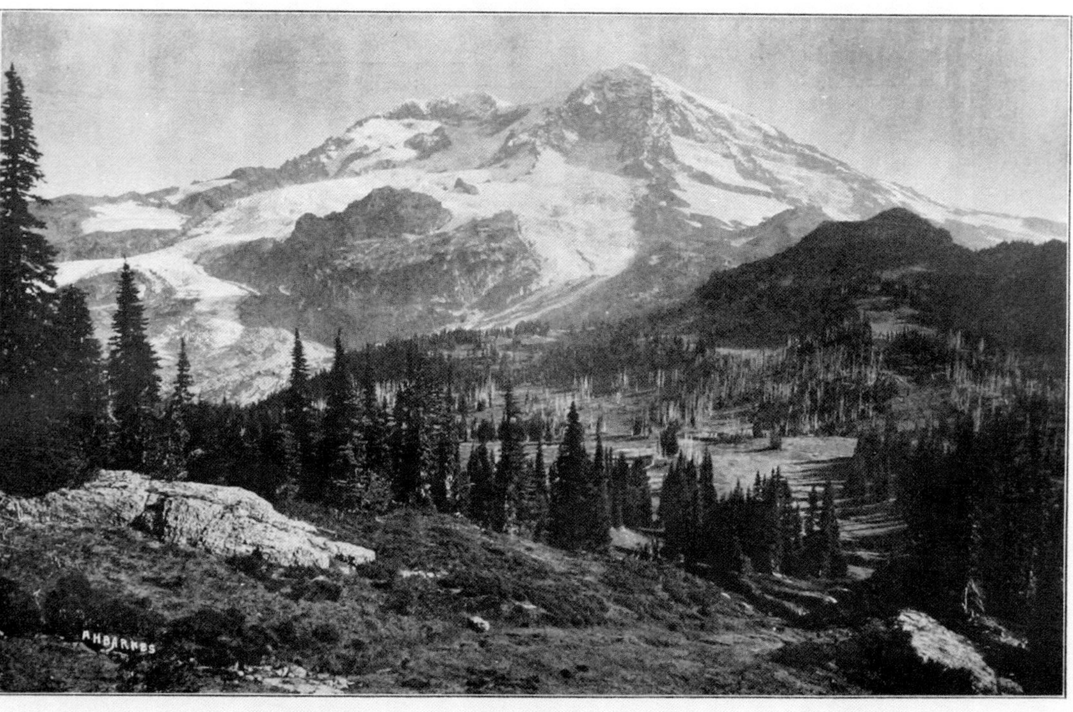

Barnes.

VIEW OF PORTION OF INDIAN HENRY'S HUNTING GROUND.
Southwest Slope of Mount Tacoma. Mountain Goat and Bear Are Sometimes Seen in This Part of the Park.

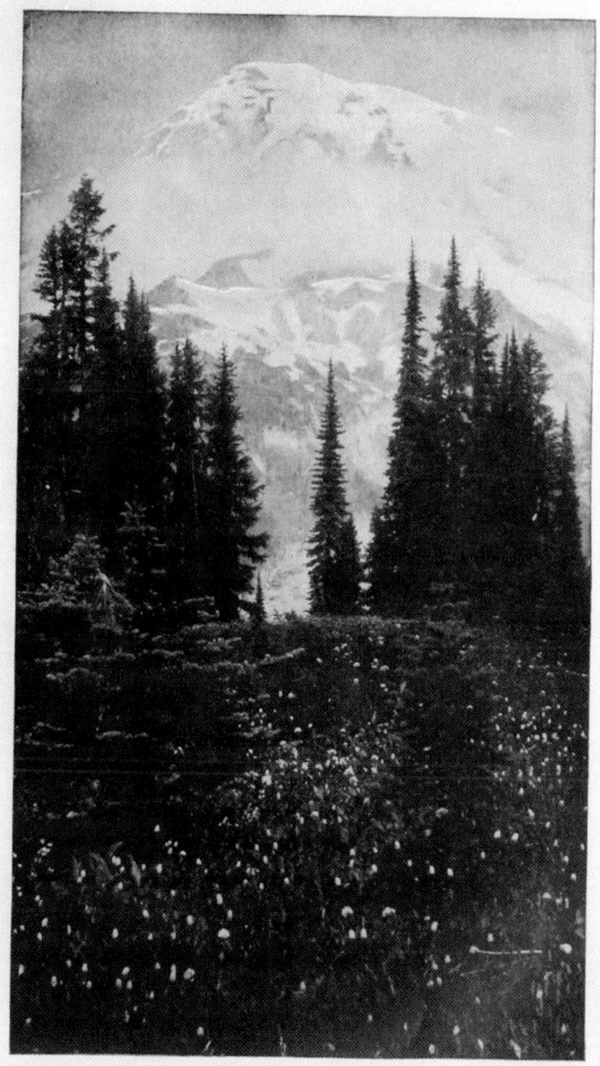

MOUNT TACOMA, FROM PARADISE PARK.

and citizens who tried to save Leschi were threatened with hanging if they stood between the mob and their victim, those same whites of the territory who, some of them, now boast that they were of the expedition that took Leschi from the fort, tied his feet under his horse, and—they will show you the spot down in the ravine of Chambers creek where they hung this patriot. "He gave his life for us, that we might keep our homes," his followers, weeping, say unto today—and the Nisqually tribe still own the lands he saved to them. Not until 1859 did the valley settlers feel safe in returning to their farms, and the future site of Tacoma remained an unbroken primeval forest until 1867.

In that year Job Carr, with his two sons, Anthony and Howard Carr, located at what is now Old Town and built the log cabin now preserved at Point Defiance park as something of great historic interest to our city. This spot, with its natural harbor, was called the place of refuge by the Puget Sound tribes, which as early as 1840 gathered annually at the head of the bay and were preached to by Archbishop Blanchard, who had planted a cross on the shore where the Northern Pacific depot is now.

Shortly after this Messrs. McCarver, Steel and Starr, of Portland, anticipating the probable site to be chosen by the Northern Pacific for its Puget Sound terminal, took up claims. The former purchased five acres of land from the Carrs and platted it, naming the place "Commencement City." In 1867 a man named Galliher came and operated the old De Lin sawmill at "Galliher's Gulch."

Naming the City.

That Tacoma is appropriately named, even as attractively as is San Francisco's "Golden Gate," is evinced by the many namesakes it has all over the country, in towns, building blocks, boats and a warship. And its name is due to Theodore Winthrop, thus:

Mr. Thomas W. Prosch, in an address before the pioneers of Pierce county, says: "On Friday, the 11th day of September, 1868, Mr. Philip Ritz landed at Steilacoom from the steamer George S. Wright. Mr. Ritz was one of the most prominent men in the territory of Washington, dwelling east of the mountains, respected and honored by all. Not only was he a scientific farmer and a man of great public spirit, but he was a reader of books, a writer, and a fluent, forceful talker. He was then on a trip acquiring information for use in the interest of the Northern Pacific Railroad Company. He wanted to see the site of their contemplated new Puget Sound town, and he also wanted to suggest a name for it. He rode over to the reservation, and from there he went by canoe to the house of the McCarvers, and later spent the night at Job Carr's. That evening and the next morning he talked with all the eloquence in him the name Tacoma. He told of a recently issued book called 'Canoe and Saddle,' which he had just read. It was, he said, written by one Theodore Winthrop.

"In this book Winthrop made known several names which, he alleged, were of Indian character, among them Kulshan, for Mount Baker; Whulge, for Puget Sound, and Tacoma, for Mount Rainier. It is only historically fair to say that these names were unknown to the white people until after the publication of this book, and unknown in our own territory until about 1866. Mr. Ritz's presentation was convincing, and General McCarver promised not only to think the matter over, but to lay it before his associates."

Mr. Carr and Mr. McCarver being entirely willing, and Mr. Starr being not unwilling, it was settled that the place should be called Tacoma. And when we consider that before Mr. Ritz's arrival the pioneers had discussed for their town the names of Washington, Pierce, Puget, Pacific, Puyallup, Rainier, Vashon, Defiance, Chebaulip and Commencement City, we feel an impulse to raise a monument to the Northern Pacific's reading emissary for rescuing us from such a fate.

In 1869 the townsite of Tacoma City was platted by McCarver, Carr and Steele. The Northern Pacific's commission visited the Sound, and, after carefully balancing the relative merits of the various terminal points suggested, selected Tacoma as possessing better natural harbor facilities and situation than the already established towns of Steilacoom, Olympia and Seattle. In a single month the population bounded from 200 to 1,000. Then came the Jay Cooke failure and delayed the new town's growth. In 1880—population 1,098—the county seat was removed to Tacoma, induced by the offers of the land company branch of the Northern Pacific. In 1880 Villard pushed on the work of the road until financial failure overtook him, and C. B. Wright, of Philadelphia came to the front and finished building the road from Hillhurst to Tacoma. In 1886 the Northern Pacific awarded the contract for piercing a tunnel at Stampede Pass to Nelson Bennett, a temporary switchback over the pass being used to connect the great East with the great West. The first train arrived on July 6 from St. Paul. It was a gala day for Tacoma, and great rejoicing was indulged in.

Then came the "boom" days, the "era of speculation." In 1890 the city had a population of 36,000. Town lots multiplied their values, worth hundreds one day and thousands the next. Then came the reaction, hastened by the panic of 1893, the Baring Brothers' failure swept the world, and it left Tacoma, so newly planted, withered down to the roots. Yet it weathered the storm as well as any other Western city, and came safely out of it, partly aided by the Klondike discovery, and locally by the wise, honest and economic city administration of Mayor Louis D. Campbell, from 1900 to 1904. Various previous administrations had exploited the city treasury, or the new town, or had been the tools of corporations, one aiding in foisting a worthless water plant on the already overburdened taxpayers for the enormous sum of $2,000,000; another was elected in the interests of the holders of nearly $2,000,000 worth of warrants, already once paid from the treasury, but being marked "not paid" by a peculiar method of its treasurer, who thus kept them in circulation, and was paid a commission on every one he sold to the banks, they were finally added to the burden of debt under which the people were already staggering. Under Mr. Campbell's administrations interest on the city's bonded indebtedness was paid for the first time; the bonds also, which had been bearing 8 and 10 per cent. interest, were taken up; $59,000 was placed in the sinking fund, the tax rate, water rates and light rates were greatly reduced, foreign corporations, power and car companies were forced to cut down exorbitant exactions and improve poor service, street paving and cement sidewalks were begun, and street car fares forced down.

The certainty of the arrival of new railroads to Tacoma has given a wonderful impetus to the city's growth. Real estate values are steady and advancing; vacant tracts are being filled with beautiful homes; the population is now estimated at 85,000, and is increasing every day.

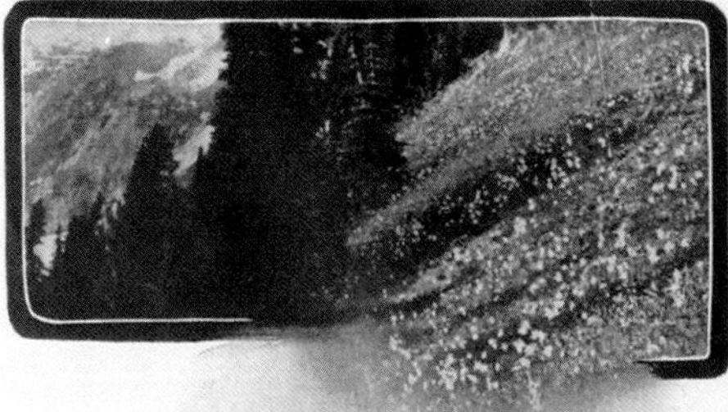

WILD FLOWERS ON SLOPES OVERLOOKING NISQUALLY GLACIER.

Tacoma made the record shipment to the Orient of 91,080 barrels of flour in a single cargo.

Tacoma is the first city of the Pacific Northwest in manufactures, and in manufacturing facilities.

ASSET OF STUPENDOUS VALUE

Hon. R. L. McCormick, Secretary of the Weyerhaeuser Company, Discusses Washington's Enormous Wealth in Timber

An estimate of the amount of standing timber in the United States and British Columbia shows:

	Feet.
North Atlantic States	5,000,000,000
Michigan, Wisconsin and Minnesota	20,000,000,000
Southern States	100,000,000,000
British Columbia	200,000,000,000
Washington	200,000,000,000
Oregon	400,000,000,000
California	200,000,000,000
Idaho and Montana	100,000,000,000
Total	1,225,000,000,000

The United States census in 1790 showed a population of 3,929,214, and in 1900 the population was 73,303,387.

The growth of fir per annum in Washington is one-eighth inch until trees arrive at maturity. The size of trees varies. Some fir, cedar and spruce in Washington grow to twelve feet in diameter at the butt of the log. The average diameter is probably six feet, and the average length two hundred feet.

In Snohomish county the Weyerhaeuser Timber Company owns a cedar tree near the Snoqualmie Falls which is over one hundred feet in circumferance. This tree must be very old, as it ranks in size with the famous "Grizzly Giant," the monarch of the California redwoods, which the writer measured some years ago, and which was one hundred and five feet in circumference and one hundred feet to the first limb, which was six feet in diameter.

The area of the state of Washington is 66,880 square miles; 42,803,200 acres. The area of Pierce county is 1,554 square miles. The estimated amount of fir, cedar, hemlock and spruce timber in the state is 200 billion feet, or one-fifth of Pacific coast timber, which in other words would be one-sixth of the total in the United States.

The timber of Washington would make a plank road three inches thick and five hundred feet wide around the world. It would load ten million cars of twenty thousand each, forty-five feet long, equal to 85,227 miles of trains. These cars would reach nearly three and a half times around the globe at the center. This timber, one inch thick, would cover as a canopy one-ninth of the state of Washington. It would cover as a canopy one inch thick and afford a floor three inches thick, all of Pierce county, Washington.

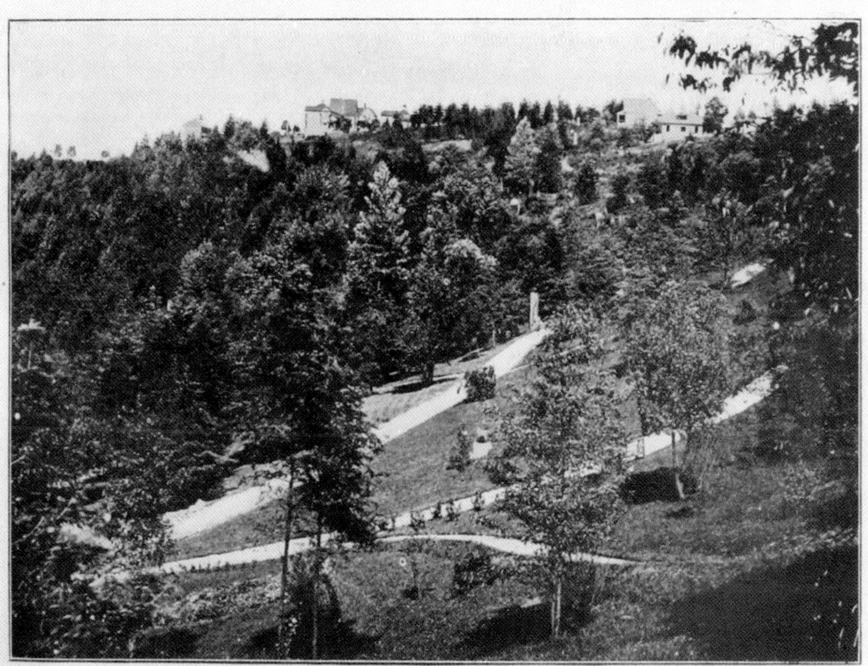

Avery. McKINLEY PARK.

A six to eight-room house for five people requires about forty thousand feet. The timber of Washington would build five million such houses, which would be sufficient to accommodate one-third of the people of the United States.

For 1906 the lumber cut in the state of Washington

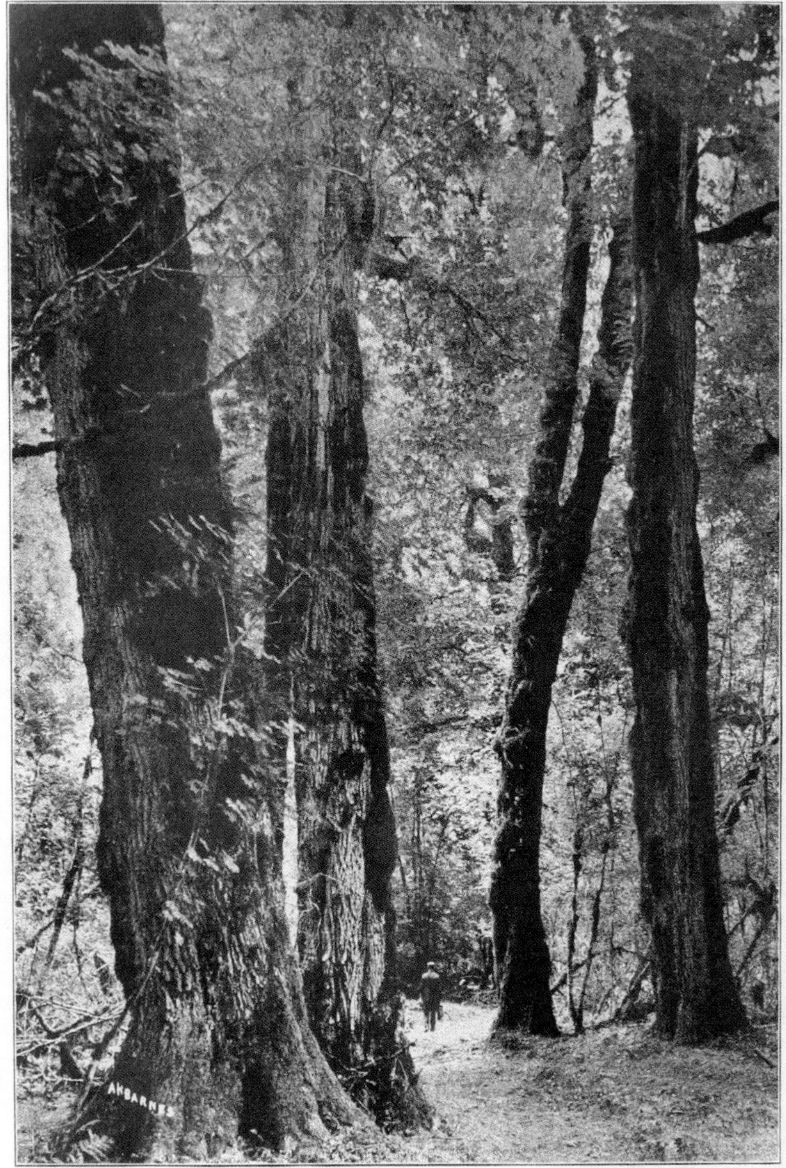

Barnes.

A TRAIL THROUGH THE SOFT MAPLES.

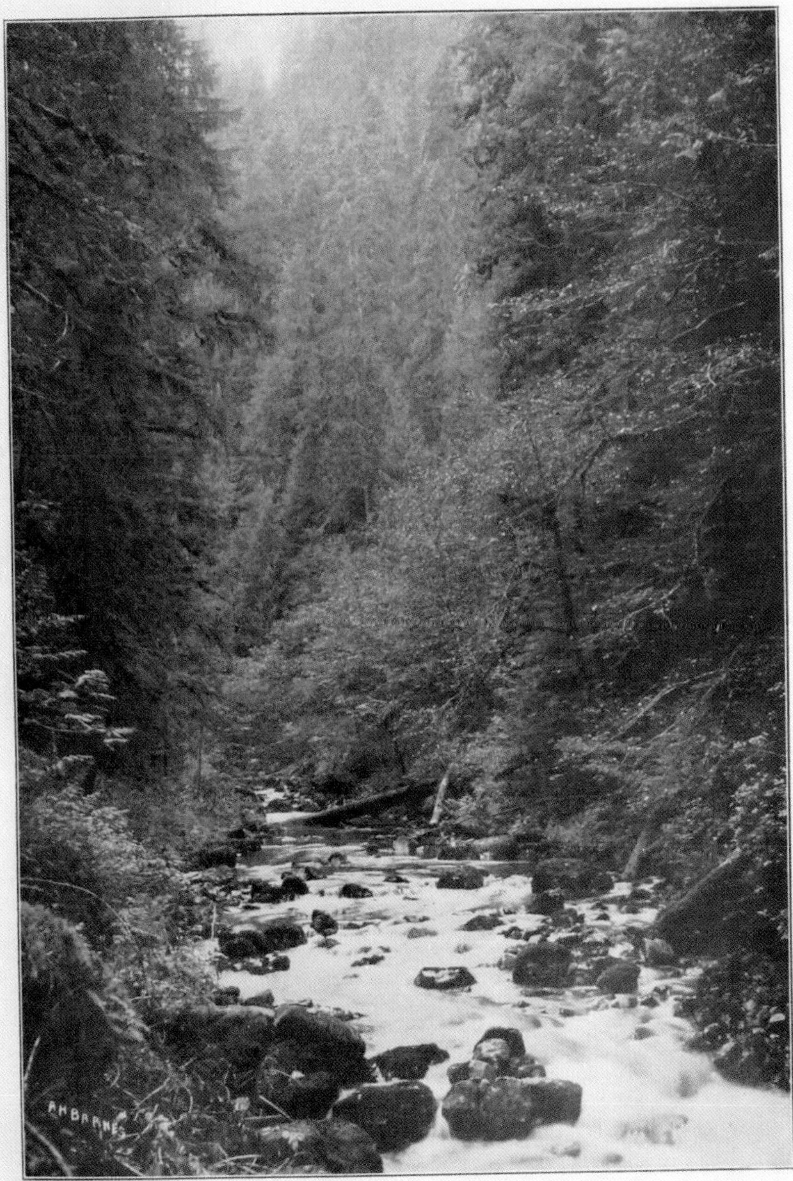

Barnes.

SOUTH FORK OF MINERAL CREEK, NEAR MOUNT TACOMA.

will probably be four billion feet at $15 market value. $60,000,000.

Cost of Production.

Expended for labor on logs, per M feet	$4.00	
Labor in sawmill, planing mill, etc.	3.50	
Labor in yards and loading	1.50	$9.00
Driving or log freight		1.50
Interest, insurance, taxes and office work ..		1.00
Value of standing timber, $1 and $2 per M ..		2.00
Profit per M feet to operator		1.50
		$15.00

The labor bill on lumber is fully two-thirds of the price at which lumber sells—at present about $10 per thousand feet, or for 1906, $40,000,000.

In order to convert Washington's 200 billion feet of standing timber into lumber, reckoning the cost to be $10 per thousand feet, the total cost would be two billion dollars for labor, and the owner of the timber would realize one-fifth for his investment.

Those who pretend to be scientific say that the Pacific coast was a wilderness of growth 4,000 years ago; that volcanic eruptions spread fires from Alaska to Southern California about 1,000 years ago, and all timber of the coast was burned except the redwoods of California, which do not burn by exposure to forest fires.

Consequently the redwood timber now standing may be said to antedate the Christian era. These magnificent forests of fir were doubtless in their prime before Columbus discovered America; before Spaniard or Russian had dreamed of the Oregon land they afterward sailed past; before Captain Gray, or Lewis and Clark, or John Jacob Astor laid the foundation claim of American discovery and occupation; before the advent of Captain Cook; before Jean de Fuca, Admiral Drake or Admiral Vancouver sailed the Pacific seas; before Admiral Wilkes explored the Pacific and chartered Puget Sound, and before Commodore Perry had opened Japan to America.

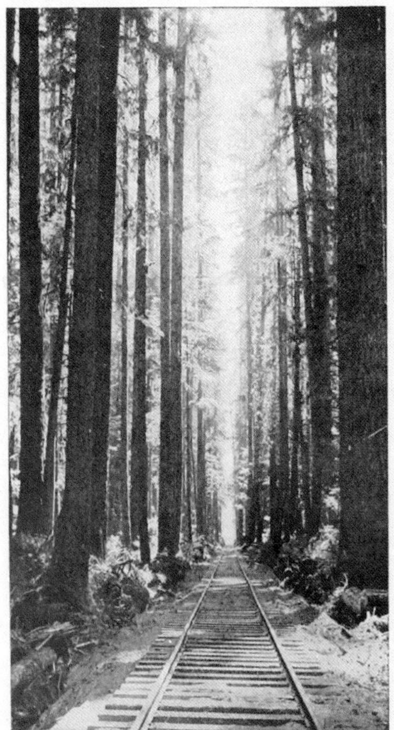

RAILROAD AVENUE, NEAR ELBE, WASH.
Courtesy Tacoma Eastern R. R.

The great white pine forests of Michigan, Wisconsin and Minnesota originally were covered by a growth estimated at 350,000,000,000 feet. Lumbering in those states began in the early 30's, but did not assume much importance until forty years later. In 1873 the cut of that district had only reached 4,000,000,000 feet. Twenty years later the cut was at its maximum, 8,500,000,000 feet. Last year, 1905, the volume of cut had dwindled to about 3,000,000,000 feet. There is probably standing timber there now not to exceed 20,000,000,000 feet. The spruce forests of Maine are almost a memory. The white pine of Pennsylvania and New York is all cut and the hemlock nearly so. The yellow pine forests of South Atlantic and contiguous states have never been estimated higher than 300,000,000,000 feet. Of this there has already been marketed fully 200,000,000,000 feet. Their annual cut of 10,000,000,000 feet will soon consume the remaining 100,000,000,000 feet. Before the 70's lumber was produced in many localities sufficient for demand, but the treeless plains of Iowa, Nebraska, Kansas and the Middle West opened for the settler, railroads made distribution possible and lumber became the commercial commodity.

In the first days timber was cut from the land of the settler or from that of his neighbor. Later, as one forest was cut, it was easy to turn to another. Today the fields of standing timber are known to be narrowing to the Pacific coast. Half a dozen to ten more years the Pacific coast will be the only source of great supply. Intelligent forestry will doubtless renew a growth of timber on lands more valuable for agriculture, but this will be a slow crop of nature.

Yellow pine in the south will, if cared for, grow to two feet in diameter in thirty years. White pine in the colder climate of the white pine reaches two feet in diameter in one hundred years, and the Pacific coast, with its mild temperature and moist climate, will produce as quickly as any country under the sun, so that we on the Pacific coast not only have today the world's timber resources, but we have the most favored locality for renewing timber growth and perpetuating for all time timber resources for all the world. The arid plains of torrid heat do not grow any timber except a limited supply of valuable hard wood. The frozen regions of the north are also barren of this growth. The future will never again see as much forest growth as is seen today.

The increased population encroaches on cut-over land for homes, for grazing, for fruit and agricultural pursuits. The increase in population increases demand normally thirty per cent every ten years. The inroads of fire in Washington, as a sample, have been ten per cent, and will continue with greater hazard as accumulating litter follows increased cutting.

The imposing of taxes will prevent private persons or companies from reforesting and waiting thirty to fifty years for a merchantable growth. We have on this coast today the timber supply for the world. None of us here present will live to see it all cut down. Improved methods of handling the product in the forest, the stream, by rail, in the sawmills and economies and saving features introduced will utilize the raw material closer, so that waste will become minimum as the value of raw material increases. If the state would take the cut-over lands of the lumberman and keep the fires out of the new growth, I believe every timber owner would turn his lands over to the state and accept for his heirs in 50 or 100 years a small percentage of what the timber and lands would then sell for, and this I believe is the only way a forest growth will be maintained to conserve the water supply at the sources of the streams.

Tacoma has regular lines of ocean steamships to China, Japan, Manila, Liverpool, Hamburg, Honolulu, South American ports, New York and Alaska.

OUR GREAT LUMBER INDUSTRY

Washington's Equipment of Mills More Extensive than than That of Any Other State in The Union

By FRANK B. COLE, Publisher West Coast Lumberman.

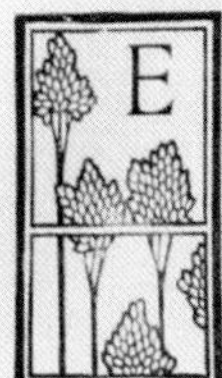

EASTERN states have grown great on agriculture; others on horticulture; others on fisheries; others on mines; others on commerce; others on lumbering. The state of Washington has within its boundaries all these great factors, which will put it some day at the head of the list of states. Eighteen years ago this state had 90,000 people; today it has 1,000,000. It is increasing more rapidly now than at any time in its history. Far above any other single industry, and perhaps greater than all other industries in the state, stands the vast lumbering interest, with its far-reaching, multiplying results.

The standing timber in the state today is estimated at 200,000,000,000 feet, worth at a fair estimate $300,000,000. Let manufacturing go on at the rate it is now progressing, and the timber will increase so much in value that at the end of twenty years the remaining timber will be worth more than it is today. One can not read the future, but unless all signs fail, this will be true fifty years hence. The protection of the timber of the state is yet in a primitive condition. The government and the state are working along hand and hand, but as yet the handling, the conservation, preservation and the propagation of the timber of Washington can not be said to have reached more than the primary lines. The policy that will protect the timber and reforest the cut-off areas will ultimately result in reproducing the forests of this state. Timber will grow under good conditions to a diameter of two feet in fifty years. This coast is peculiarly favored in the fact that its timber reproduces itself. All it wants is the opportunity. It is thought by some that the timber today is reproducing itself faster than it is cut off for manufacturing.

Economy in the manufacturing of lumber is not a marked feature. It has not yet reached the point where any fair-minded man can truthfully say that there is no useless waste. The stranger that visits the mills and the logging camps of the state is shocked by the useless waste and extravagant methods of manufacturing. Today, however, at least one-third to one-half more lumber is manufactured from a given timber area than was manufactured fifteen or twenty years ago from an equal area. It was but a few years ago that, in the buying and selling of timber, hemlock was not considered of value. Today it is known as one of the best timbers that grow, and in the market it is regularly quoted at high figures, while as an interior finish it has no equal. Fir, however, stands pre-eminently the king of the forest. It practically grows everywhere in Western Washington. On one acre carefully cruised has been found 300,000 feet of it, while occasional sections have cruised 60,000,000 to 70,000,000 feet. The ordinary mind can not conceive what these big figures stand for. They appeal to a man like the great figures so flippantly used in the financial statements of great corporations or government statistics. If the lumber of Washington could be today manufactured and put on the market at once, it would bring to its owners from $300,000,000 to $400,000,000. There are in the state of Washington over 1,000 plants engaged in the manufacture of lumber and shingles; there are 180 logging roads, besides perhaps 4,000 logging engines at work bringing in its timber.

The mills of this state will manufacture during the year 1906 approximately 4,000,000,000 feet of lumber and 7,000,000,000 shingles. The value of this enormous output will not be far from $70,000,000. A great per cent. of this vast sum comes to the state from outside territory, or, in other words, it is foreign money brought into this commonwealth. It brings, on an average, to each man, woman

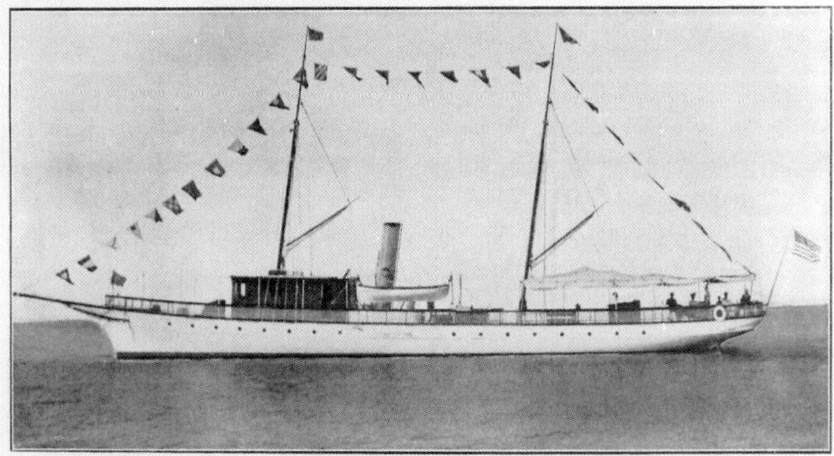

STEAM YACHT "EL PRIMERO"

Trim Craft Owned by Chester Thorne, President of the National Bank of Commerce.

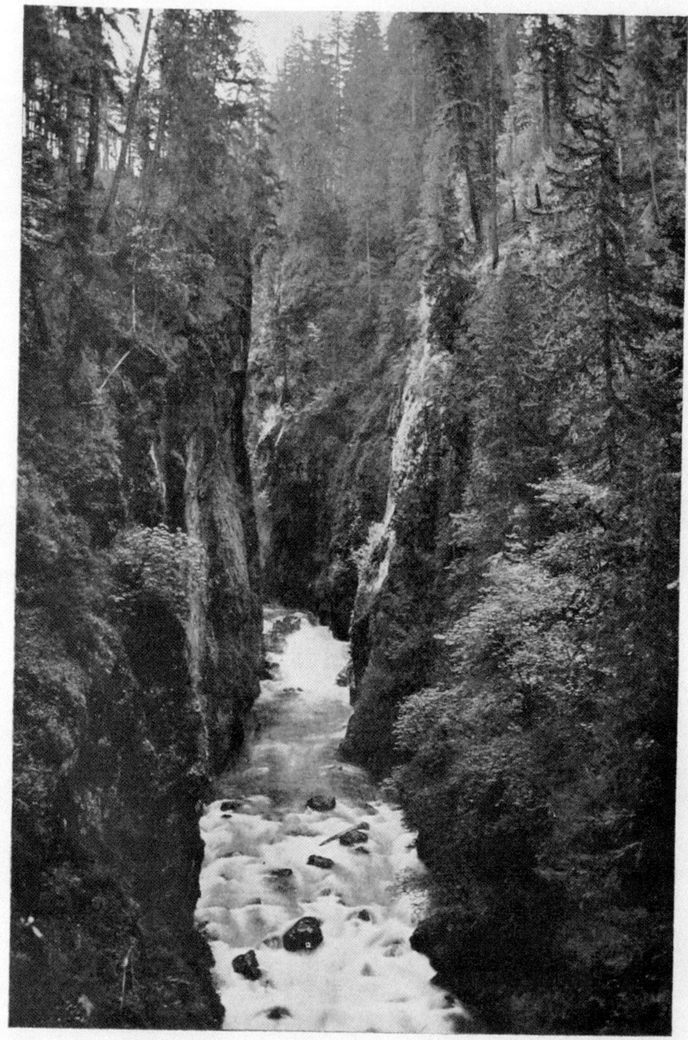

Barnes. VIEW OF NISQUALLY CANYON FROM A POINT 300 FEET ABOVE THE RIVER.

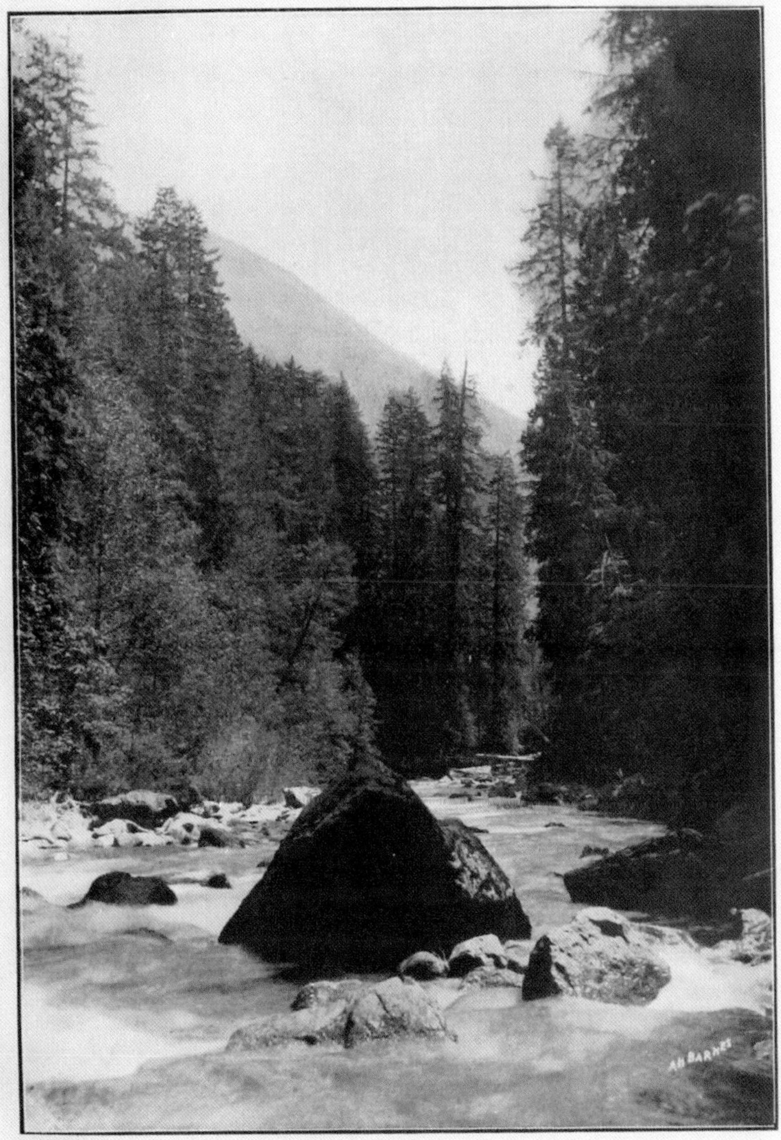

Barnes. VIEW DOWN UPPER SKOKOMISH RIVER, ABOVE LAKE CUSHMAN.

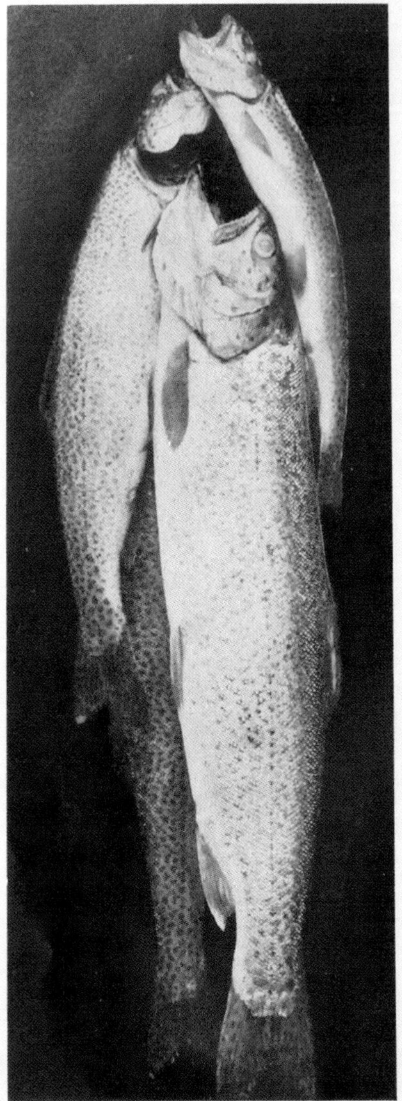

MOUNTAIN TROUT FROM MASHELL RIVER.

and child in the state, $70, an amount per capita that is exceeded perhaps in no other state from natural resources, excepting the state of Montana, where its fabulous mines bring untold millions to its limited population.

There are two great central manufacturing points that stand out prominently in the lumber industry in the state of Washington. Ballard is the leading shingle manufacturing town of the world. It has no rival, though Whatcom county is the greatest shingle manufacturing county in the state. Tacoma has the largest lumber cutting capacity of any city in the world. The Tacoma Mill Company holds the record of having cut more lumber in a day than any other mill. In one day of ten hours it manufactured 467,866 feet. Since it began manufacturing in 1868 it has turned out over 2,000,000,000 feet of lumber.

The St. Paul & Tacoma Lumber Company has an annual product exceeding in value that of any other mill company on the Coast, while the same may be said of the output of sash and doors from the great plant of the Wheeler-Osgood Company. During the past year several new mills have been added to Tacoma's list, while the output of others has been increased. Not included in Tacoma's list of mills is a large number of mills that pay tribute to this city, and which add largely to the volume of lumber business and the general trade. Among the many factors that have contributed to the lumber industry of this locality, the Tacoma Eastern railroad deserves pre-eminence. Along its one hundred miles of tracks a large number of mills have sprung into existence, which market their product largely through Tacoma.

The advent of other railroads into the state of Washington will open up new fields for lumbering, widen the market, and make this state a greater factor in the lumber markets of the world. It has been held by many that manufacturing lumber in this state will double within ten years, though it is quite probable, however, that the manufacturing of shingles has practically reached the limit. So many substitutes for shingles are now on the market that the demand is not increasing with the population. The shingle manufacturer of the state is obliged to curtail his output, and at times suspend entirely the manufacture of shingles until there is a demand for them. This year would have been phenomenal in the manufacturing of lumber but for the inability of transportation companies to care for the traffic. Lumbermen have suffered untold losses by the inadequate service rendered by the transcontinental railroads. In spite of this drawback, however, the year has been an active one. Local demand and the excessive call from California have absorbed large amounts of lumber manufactured in this state, and in a way offset the loss occasioned by car shortage.

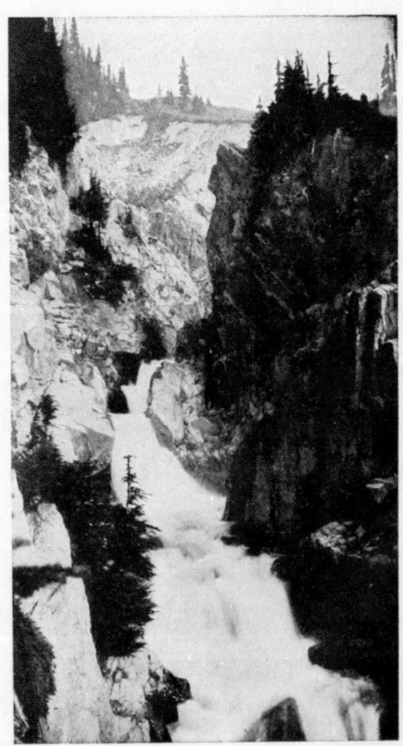

HEADWATERS OF PARADISE RIVER.
Courtesy Tacoma Eastern R. R.

TACOMA'S EDUCATIONAL ADVANTAGES

Unequalled by Any Other City in the Northwest — Excellent Public School System and Many Private Institutions of Learning.

By ALBERT H. YODER, Superintendent Tacoma City Schools.

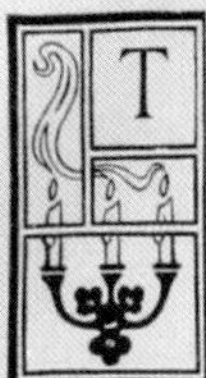

HE educational facilities of Tacoma are the equal of most cities of 100,000. There is a well-organized system of public schools, and an unusual number of private ones. The city has two large Catholic academies, a Lutheran academy, an excellent boys' boarding school, three large business colleges, the Annie Wright seminary for young ladies, one of the best of its kind in the West; Whitworth college (Presbyterian), and the University of Puget Sound (Methodist), in the center of the best residence district; a large Indian school in the suburbs, two hospital training schools for nurses, a summer normal school for school teachers, now in its twelfth year; the Y. M. C. A. and Y. W. C. A. night schools, with special work for employed people, and a number of private schools conducted by various denominations.

There are 263 teachers employed in the public school system, and more than 10,000 children enrolled. The course is divided into 12 years, eight in the elementary school, and four in the High school.

There are 26 schools in the city, including the recently established Parental school, where boys of compulsory school age, without good homes, or incorrigible in school, are given special training in the usual branches, gymnastics, and manual training. The Grammar schools are of good size, most of them employing a supervising principal, but are not crowded. For example: The enrollment of some of them for the past month is:

Bryant	616
Central	795
Edison	670
Emerson	520
Grant	533
Hawthorne	701
Logan	602
Lowell	550
Grant	572

Special supervisors are provided for the work in music and in drawing. There is also special supervision of the primary grades. The course of study is similar to that obtaining in other cities of the same size.

In September the High school moved into the beautiful new building, the best model of school architecture in the Northwest, and only equaled in the West by the new High school of Los Angeles, California This building has been fitted with the best furniture, designed especially for the school, and equipped with the best laboratory facilities. In addition to the usual laboratories in physics, chemistry, biology, botany, etc., there is a laboratory devoted to physical geography, the equipment of which is the best in the West. There is also a strong commercial department, with a four years' course of study. The gymnasium is 28x104 feet, thoroughly equipped with the best apparatus, and provided with lockers, dressing rooms, and shower baths. There are two instructors in physical culture, one for boys, and one for girls.

The manual training department has a four-year course for both boys and girls, the boys taking the usual work in wood, iron and cabinet-making, and the girls, cooking and sewing. There are 38 teachers and 1100 students in the High school. Every student is required to take four years in English, at least two years of some other language, two years of science, one biological and one physical, and two years of mathematics and two of history. The balance of the course is elective. Sixteen units are required for graduation.

The usual student activities are maintained—athletics, football, baseball, track and other sports, basket ball and tennis, debating societies, a cadet corps, a school paper, etc.

People coming from other cities will find the school opportunity for children, or for special work in private schools or colleges, as good as that maintained in most of the cities in the East. Tacoma, as other Western cities, aspires to maintain as good educational facilities as can be found elsewhere.

Tacoma's foreign exports exceed those of all the other twelve ports of this district combined, including Seattle.

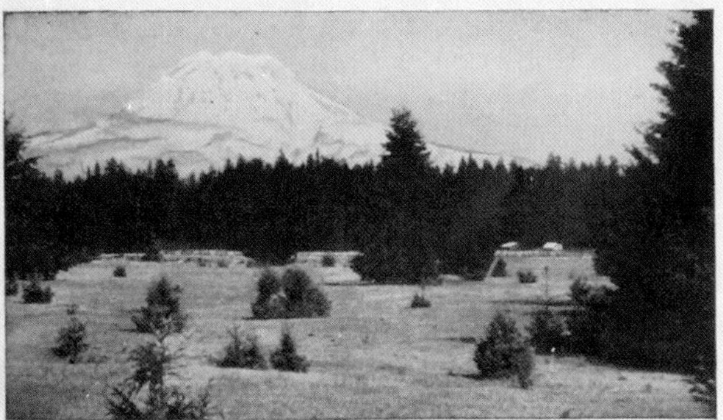

MAHON'S PRAIRIE, WITH MOUNT TACOMA'S SNOW-CAPPED PEAK IN THE DISTANCE.

Grant. Edison. Central.

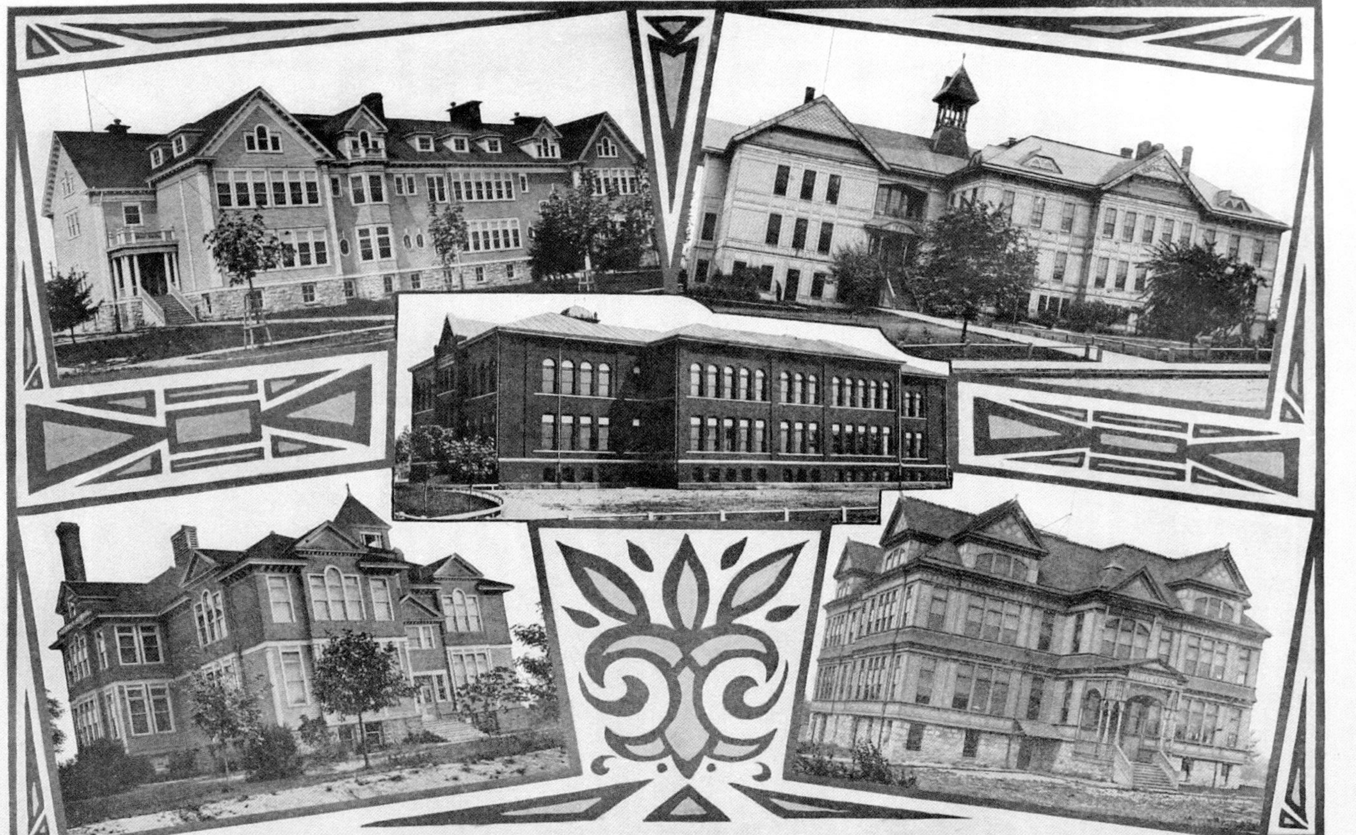

Avery. Sherman. Irving.

FIVE OF TACOMA'S SCHOOLS.

SANDERS CO. ST. L.

Avery.

RESIDENCE OF L. T. DEMPSEY
Corner Division Avenue and South M Street.

RESIDENCE OF G. L. GOWER
417 North E Street.

RESOURCES OF WONDERFUL REGION

Vast Wealth and Incomparable Scenic Beauty Along Line of Tacoma Eastern Railway

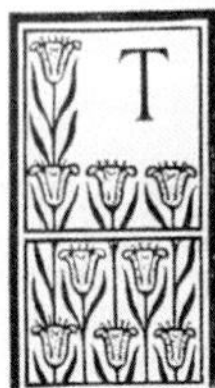

THE Tacoma Eastern railroad passes through a section of Washington's richest country, famed for its vast natural resources and advantages, as well as its incomparable scenic beauty. Lumbering is the great source of wealth, the immense forests of fir, cedar, spruce, hemlock and other valuable woods furnishing material for shingle, lumber, and planing mills along the road as well as at Tacoma, giving employment to hundreds of men, as this great reserve is being drawn on to supply the markets of the world.

Million Feet of Logs Per Day.

It is only a few years since the Tacoma Eastern was first projected into this region. At first the giants of the forests were felled to supply the mills at Tacoma, but with the constant pushing forward of the road into this virgin territory, the natural and other advantages so appealed to the mill owner and investor that today there are twenty-six saw and shingle mills, with a daily cut of nearly 700,000 feet of lumber and 1,000,000 shingles, located along this line. The demand of these mills, as well as the mills in Tacoma, swell the daily log cut to nearly one and one-quarter million feet. While these figures must appear to the average reader as enormous, still the impression made in this great reserve can hardly be noticed, so great is the supply.

Growing and Prosperous Towns.

As the railroad was extended, mills were built, and the forest near the rails cleared. Laborers were brought in, then came homeseekers, merchants and professional men, who formed the nucleus for the towns that now show prosperity and growth at numerous points on the line. Other thriving industries have found place beside the busy saw and shingle mills, and the valleys and logged-off lands of almost inexhaustible fertility are blossoming through the efforts of the agriculturist and horticulturist, who find it easy to raise profitable crops of grain, hops, fruits and vegetables—in fact, almost anything that can be grown in the temperate zone.

Agriculture and Horticulture.

Berries and other small fruits thrive, especitlly in the valleys, and bear most prolific crops, ripening, however, slightly later than near the Sound, where the full benefit of the warm Japan current is felt. The soil of the valleys is suitable for hops, which average a ton per acre. Hay yields two crops a year, the first from three to four tons, and the second two tons an acre. From 250 to 350 bushels an acre is the yield of potatoes, while carrots and other root crops, including sugar beets, average from 30 to 40 tons. Oats cut about 90 bushels to the acre, while wheat, which is raised chiefly for feed, averages from 40 to 50 bushels per acre.

Rich Mineral Deposits.

In the Cascades is gold-bearing copper pyrites ore, while silver and lead are to be found in paying quantities, and some valuable mines are being worked. Extending along the base of the Cascade mountains, nearly the entire distance from the Columbia river to the British line, is one of the most extensive coal fields in the world, and it is only just beginning to be developed. In quality this coal varies from light to a heavy bituminous. While some is well adapted for making gas and coke, other varieties are excellent for domestic use and steaming purposes.

A Ready Market at Tacoma.

Tacoma, lying at the head of Commencement Bay, is the headquarters and western terminus of the Tacoma Eastern railroad. Thousands of acres of land with water frontage afford terminal facilities for any number of railroads, and the deep sea-going ships, which register from ports all over the globe. In addition to the Northern Pacific railway, which makes this point its principal terminus, several other transcontinental lines are building west to take advantage of these exceptional facilities at Tacoma. Thus distribution to the markets of the world is afforded the products of the region reached by the Tacoma Eastern railroad.

Pierce's County's Varied Resources.

Pnerce county, which the Tacoma Eastern traverses, already has a population of more than 125,000, with resources as varied as its topography, which rises from sea level at Tacoma to the top of Mt. Tacoma, the greatest volcanic glacial peak in the Northwest—14,528 feet high. Numerous streams, which are fed by the great glaciers on the mountain, afford unlimited horse-power for the generation of electricity. About two-thirds of the area of the county is covered with forests of fir, spruce, cedar, ash, maple, alder, with some oak and cottonwood.

Out From Tacoma.

From the station in Tacoma, to the south, the rails lie through a portion of the manufacturing section of the city. Beyond Bismarck, at the city limits, are numerous small ranches or farms, whose owners have cleared the ground and are growing fruit and vegetables, and raising poultry. Dairying is also successfully carried on, especially in the Clover Creek valley, ten miles out, where rich meadows grow on alluvial soil. Between Tacoma and Kapowsin, 23 miles out, and included in the latter town, are nine saw mills, three shingle mills and one planing mill.

$3,000,000 Electrical Plant.

On a spur, extending two miles from Kapowsin, at Electron, is the plant of the Puget Sound Power company, the building of which has involved the expenditure of $3,000,000. With an ultimate capacity of 40,000 horse-power, one-half that energy has been developed. This affords cheap electrical power and light, which have been a large factor in the development of Tacoma and the surrounding cities.

Lumbering and Gardening.

Kapowsin, at the lower end of Lake Kapowsin, is a mill town, as is Lakehead, at the upper end. From Lakehead on, the road passes through the fertile Ohop valley, where, in season, hops, fruit and vegetables are grown in profusion. Lumbering is also carried on through there to some extent, especially around Ohop lake, five mills being located at Lakehead, Ohop, Skewis and Eatonville.

Picturesque Scenery, Hunting and Fishing.

From Eatonville, the line passes through splendid forests and the country becomes more rugged. Not far from Eatonville are several gold prospects, a deposit of fine silica and an immense ledge of mineral paint. At LaGrande, thirty-seven miles from Tacoma, the road enters the Nisqually canyon, with its perpendicular walls hundreds of feet high. The scenery for several miles along the road from here is most grand, the Nisqually river, far below the track, rushing and tumbling over the rocks, wasting thousands of horse-power that before long will be utilized for the generation of electricity. Numerous streams along this portion of the road afford fine trout fishing, while in the hills are found deer, grouse, bear, cougar and other game. At Alder and Elbe are six shingle mills, the latter town being in the center of the Succotash valley, a fertile bottom well adapted to farming and fruit growing.

Mineral Lake—Lumbering and Mining Arsenic.

Three miles from Elbe, at Park Junction, the line turns south, crossing the Nisqually river into Lewis county. For four miles the road winds through a magnificent forest of fir and cedar, some of the trees being immense in size, ranging up to 14 feet in diameter and to a height of 200 feet, without a limb to mar their symmetrical beauty. There are several hotels at Mineral, which is becoming noted as a summer resort, while the lake and streams flowing into it afford fine sport and heavy creels of trout. Two mills are located there. An exceedingly rich deposit of realgar, or arsenic, is bing mined and smelted near this point.

Coal Mining.

Four miles away, on a branch, are the Ladd coal mines, where a fine quality of steam coal is being taken out. Here the railroad secures its supply of fuel for motive power.

Rich Big Bottom Country.

From mineral the line has been built through Watkins to Tilton, a distance of 60 miles from Tacoma, and is being rapidly extended into the famed territory known as the Big Bottom country, comprising some 100,000 acres in the Cowlitz, Rainy and Cispus valleys in eastern Lewis county. Here the soil is exceedingly rich, being an alluvial deposit mixed with volcanic ash.

Unusual Opportunieies.

Away from the bottom lands it is more or less mountainous and is covered with fine timber. In addition to coal, copper, gold and silver, fire and other clays are being taken from the hills. The principal agricultural products of this country are wheat, oats, barley, hops, hay and vegetables. Cattle, hogs and poultry are raised and dairying is carried on profitably. Unusual opportunities for making money in any of these lines are open to anybody.

Wonderland of the Cascades.

From Park Junction, a branch of the Tacoma Eastern extends to Ashford, the eastern terminus of the road, where the stage is taken for Longmire Springs and Mount Tacoma, the "Wonderland of the Cascades," with its great glaciers, beautiful waterfalls and lakes, and grand and rugged scenery, equaling, it is said by travelers, that of the Yosemite valley and the Yellowstone National park.

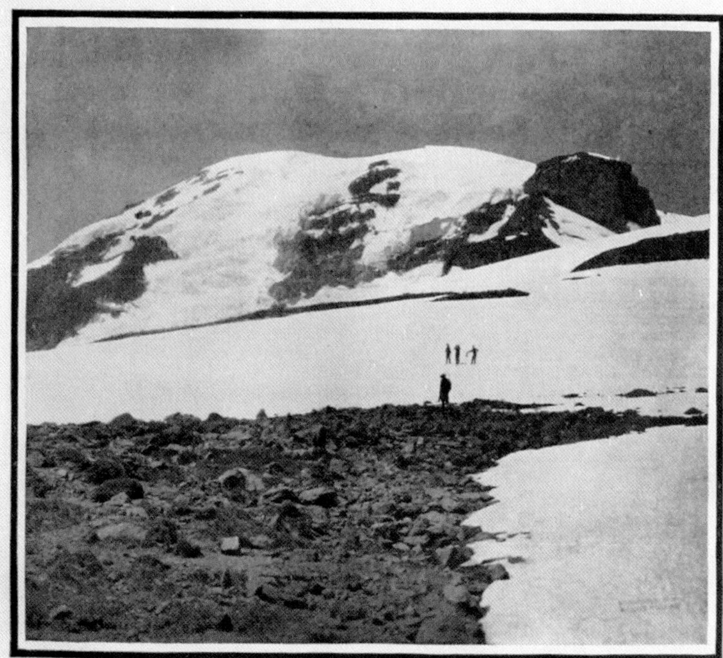

SNOW FIELDS ABOVE ALTA VISTA — GIBRALTAR ROCK IN DISTANCE.
Courtesy Tacoma Eastern R. R.

S. M. Jackson.   Arthur J. Prichard.

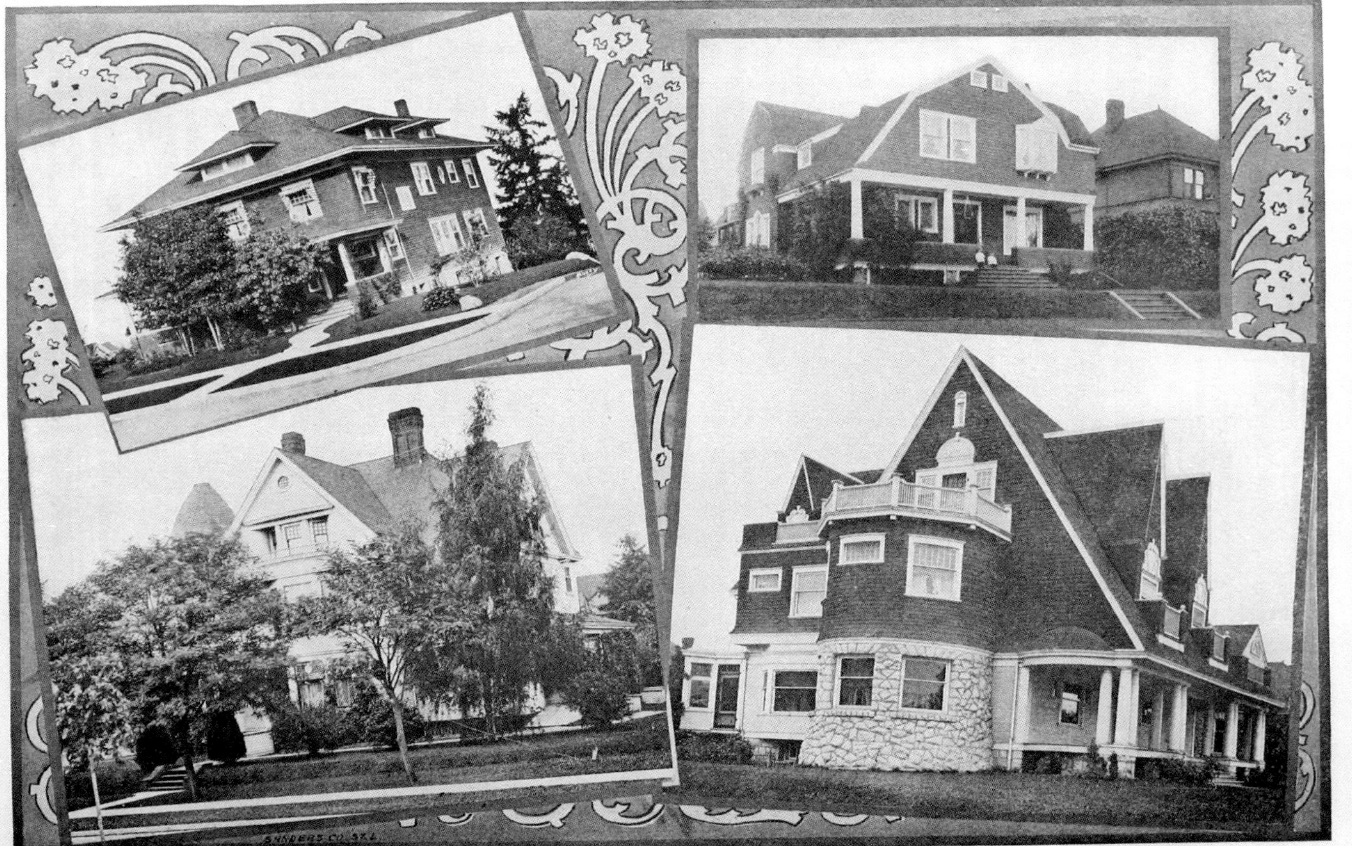

Avery.   George B. Kandle.   F. H. Murray.

Herman Klaber. Charles H. Hyde.

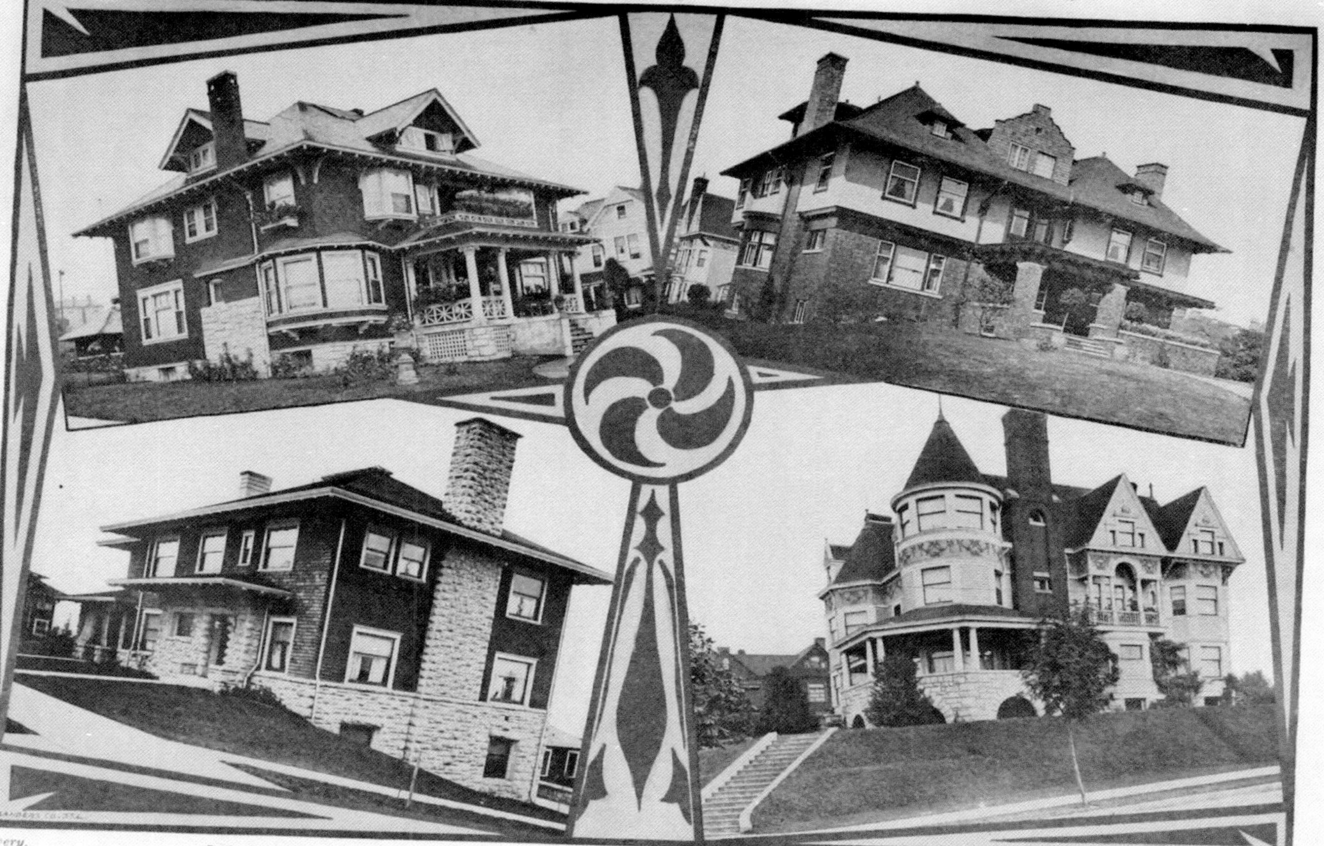

Avery. R. S. Grosscup. Richard Vaeth.

COLLECTION OF REPRESENTATIVE TACOMA RESIDENCES.

WASHINGTON'S MINERAL RESOURCES

Many Promising Mining Districts, With Bright Outlook in Production of Precious Metals — Greatest Coal Measures in the West.

OF WASHINGTON'S four great primal resources—the forests, the fields, the fisheries and the mines—the last remains an asset about which there is the least definite knowledge, with the largest amount of speculation. There are a few elements of certainty in the situation, however. The state is centrally situated within the mineral zone. The mountain range that intersects it from north to south is part of a chain that has yielded untold wealth of precious metals from Alaska, through California, and on to the southward, while geologists and experienced prospectors who have carefully examined into the situation aver that the vein has not faulted, and that Washington will ultimately take her place among the leading producing states, with this important interest ranking well up with lumbering and agriculture in its contribution.

Up to this time mining operations have been carried forward under serious drawbacks, due to the fact that the mountain fastnesses of the state are comparatively inaccessible, and it has been practically impossible to secure transportation facilities for material and machinery to properties already discovered in order to work them upon a scale sufficiently large to produce results, or to freight the ores to smelters for reduction. This obstacle has likewise served to prevent systematic prospecting, and developments have necessarily been retarded. The difficulty, however, will soon be largely overcome. The construction of 2,000 miles of additional railway trackage within the state will be accompanied by the completion of a comprehensive system of highways that will allow of the exploitation of mineral deposits upon a scale which will soon demonstrate the real worth of this interest.

There are a number of districts within the state which have already established themselves as producers of merit. Prominent among these is the Mount Baker district in Whatcom county, where $2,500,000 has been invested in development work, stamp mills and the necessary equipment for mining upon a representative scale. Commensurate results are being obtained in the output of free milling ores, while to the southward there are many districts of rich promise. Snohomish county has a half dozen districts under development, shipping their products to the smelter at Everett, while there are seven mining districts in Pierce county, and extending over into King and Kittitas counties, in which discoveries have been made, though insufficient development work has not permitted of the establishment of their capacity. Placer gold has been taken from the streams of Kittitas and Ferry counties for nearly a half century, and the product is still maintained at its pristine volume, with considerable improved machinery recently added to facilitate work. Several fine properties of proved worth have been developed into productive mines in Okanogan and Stevens counties, demonstrating the presence of workable ore bodies both east and west of the Cascades, while there are indications of rich mineral resources in the Olympic range, to the west of Puget Sound, that await the opening up of the peninsula to settlement.

While the ultimate future of the mining of precious metals cannot at this time be foretold with accuracy, there is no doubt as to Washington's eminence in mining. Her vast coal measures are already contributing from their storehouses a splendid revenue, and are serving to give precedence to the state from a commercial and industrial standpoint. No other commonwealth on the Pacific slope produces coal in merchantable quantities, and the element of cheap fuel gives an unquestioned preeminence in manufacturing and shipping operations.

For a time the coal mining industry was retarded because of the increased use of oil from the California fields for fuel purposes, and the establishment of immense electrical power plants, but during 1906 there was a marked revival, and the output was increased more than 25 per cent over the previous year, with a total product exceeding 3,500,000 tons, worth more than $11,000,000 at tidewater. The increase in demand was due to consumption throughout the Pacific Northwest, the capacity of working properties being taxed to suply the requirements, with bright prospects for extending the output very materially in the future.

The mines of the Northwestern Improvement company at Roslyn and Cle Elum are the largest on the coast, producing nearly one-half of the output credited to this state, while there are fine working properties in Pierce and King counties, the former producing an excellent coking coal, with over 100 ovens in operation.

Extensive lime deposits in San Juan and Island counties are the basis of a large industry. The cement rock in Skagit and Whatcom counties has attracted hundreds of thousands of dollars in capital in their development within the past two years. The iron ores of the state remain to be brought to the producing stage, though several millions of dollars is being expended in the establishment of iron and steel works, and capitalists are acquiring properties which give promise of placing this interest upon a paying basis of great worth to the Pacific coast, where millions of dollars are annually sent abroad in the importation of iron and steel. Large sandstone quarries are worked at Tenino and Chuckanut, with marble deposits in Spokane and Stevens counties, while many deposits of clay adapted to the manufacture of drain tile sewer pipe, vitrified paving blocks and brick, in various sections of the state give the baser metals a present worth of inestimable value.

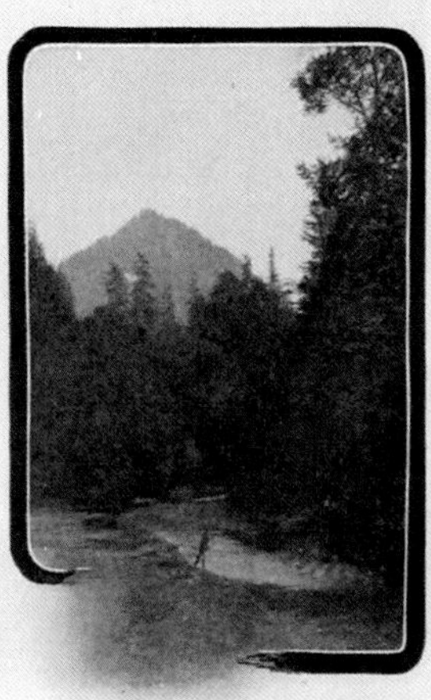

TROUT FISHING IN MINERAL CREEK.

FISHERIES A THRIVING INDUSTRY

Famous Waterways Provide a Wealth of Sea Foods — Washington Leads in Fishing, for Profit or Pleasure

Sea foods of infinite variety and incalculable value contribute to the precedence of Washington among the states. Her commercial fisheries are unapproached, while a wealth of species of the finny tribe adds to her attractions for the sportsman. Equally famed for great canneries and takings of thousands of salmon for market purposes, and for splendid trout streams, Washington waters are an important element in enhancing industrial activity and adding to the pleasure of her inhabitants.

Fishing as an industry affords employment to more than 10,000 people during the season of active operations, and for 1906 the disbursement for wages alone amounted to $3,024,795. There is a permanent investment of $7,831,130 in the industry, and the product of last year amounted in value to $7,175,614. Of this total, Puget Sound showed returns of $5,584,705; the Columbia river, $1,311,321; Grays Harbor, $132,180, and Willapa harbor, $147,318. Salmon takes the lead in the extent and value of productions, the various canneries of the state making a pack of half a million cases during the year, to the value of $2,607,360, while more than $2,000,000 worth of this splendid fish were sold in the fresh state and either put in cold storage or cured for market.

The output for the year was materially lessened from the previous season, due to the fact of its being the "off" year in the run of sockeyes, which are the leading merchantable fish taken in the waters of Puget Sound, this species coming in flood tide only once in four years, when the total fisheries output is in excess of $10,000,000. Of other varieties of commercial fisheries, the cod family is prominent, the annual takings being very extensive, while large fleets of vessels are operated from Puget Sound in Alaskan waters, bringing their catches here for curing. The Pacific cod is rapidly making for itself a market throughout the country, extending clear to the Atlantic seaboard. It is pronounced equal in quality to the Newfoundland product, and the basis of a great industry has been laid in its curing and distribution.

Millions of pounds of halibut are annually brought to Puget Sound from the north and shipped in refrigerator cars to every portion of the United States, while an immense export trade is being developed in fisheries products, Europe being a large consumer of canned and cured salmon, the excellent quality of the product and its economy as a food supply giving it high favor in the markets of the world.

Deep sea fishing, however, will soon find a rival in the shell fisheries of the state. The oyster industry has already established for itself an important place, while through systematic cultivation it is susceptible of a development which will ultimately accord to it first place in this important interest. There are great areas suitable to oyster culture throughout the state, while this toothsome bivalve thrives exceptionally. Native oysters have been marketed for many years, and, though small, have established for themselves a demand in excess of the supply. The planting of eastern oysters is of recent date, but has been attended with such successful results that more than one hundred carloads of seed oysters are now being imported annually, and these will soon be yielding a revenue of great worth. The present center of cultivation of eastern oysters is in Willapa Harbor, but experiments have demonstrated that they will thrive, attain a larger size than in their native waters, and retain their flavor in Puget Sound and Grays Harbor.

Equipped with a spade, the camper on almost any of Washington's splendid beaches may provide a bucketful of delicious clams in a few moments, and the larger proportion of the product of this variety of shell fish is thus consumed, though thousands of dollars' worth are annually marketed, and one large cannery is maintained, shipping a considerable quantity to points outside the state.

The last year crabs to the value of $30,000, and a quarter of a million pounds of shrimps, valued at $35,000, figured as a commercial product.

The state maintains a system of artificial hatcheries for replenishing the supply of salmon, more than 50,000,000 fry having been turned into Washington waters last year, while two hatcheries operated by the national government added 25,000,000 more. One trout hatchery produced 1,000,000 fish in 1906.

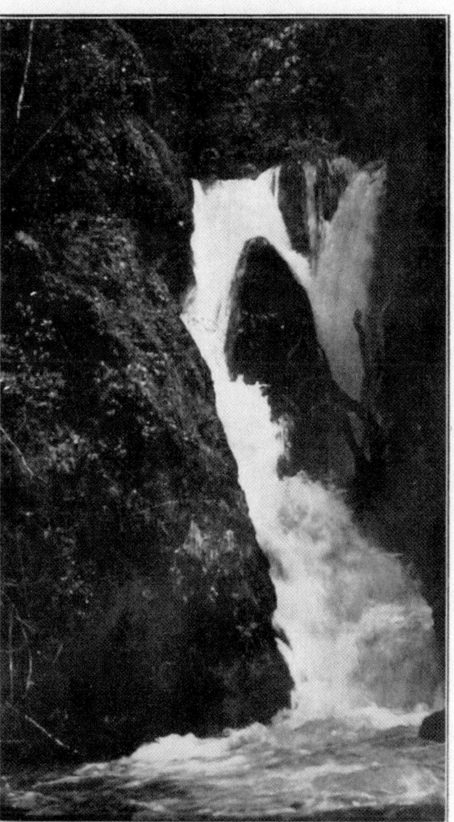

FAIRY FALLS, STEVENS CANYON. Barnes.

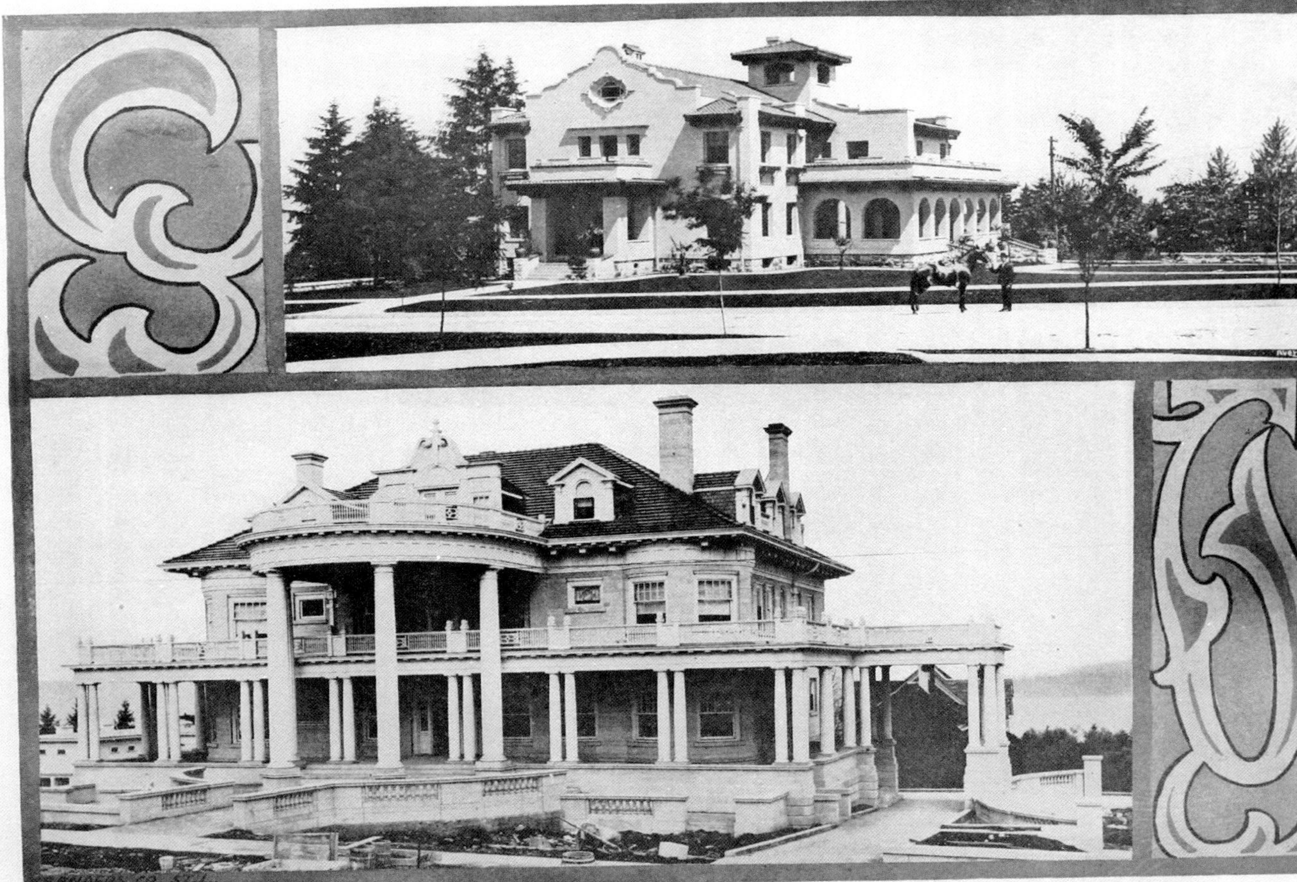

Avery.

LOWER PICTURE—RESIDENCE OF W. R. RUST, JUST COMPLETED.

UPPER PICTURE—RESIDENCE OF W. F. SHEARD.

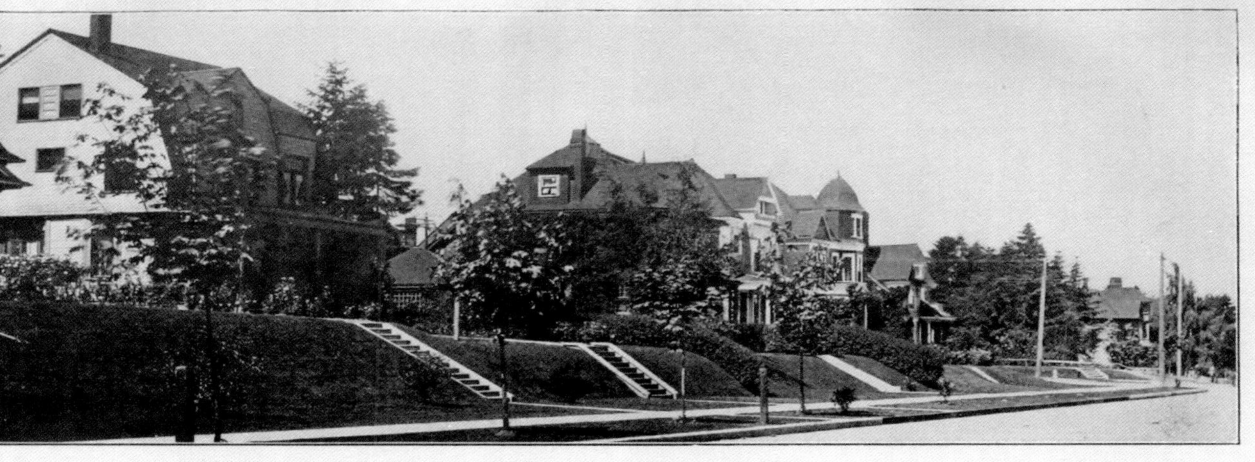

Avery.

West Side North Yakima Avenue, Looking North from Fifth.

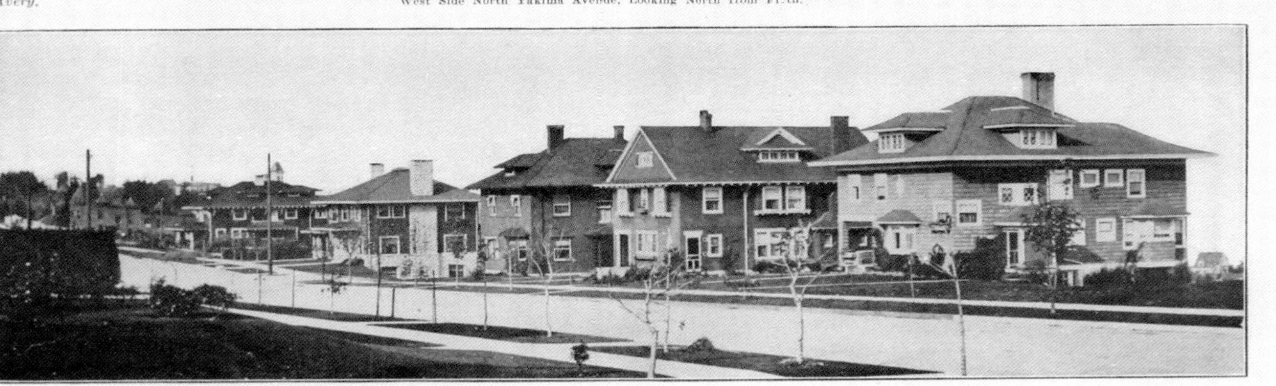

Avery.

East Side North Yakima Avenue, Looking North from Sixth.

VIEWS OF TWO BLOCKS IN A BEAUTIFUL RESIDENCE SECTION.

A TRIP TO THE TOP OF MOUNT TACOMA

By JAMES A. SPROULE.

Visitors to the Northwest and, especially, Tacoma cannot fail to be impressed with a view of the mighty eminence from which the City of Destiny derived its name. There is always something fascinating about the grand old mountain, whether in summer, when it reflects the setting sun and turns from red to rose and then to bluish white, or in winter, when the rising sun bursts in splendor over the adjacent foothills, and more especially in those few short days in midwinter when Old Sol starts the day from over the highest point of the mountain itself. Then again, in early fall, when the smoke and the haze from the valleys have obscured the foothills, and only the upper part is visible, apparently floating in a sea of vapor, it seems that it truly deserves its Indian name, Tahoma—near to the eternal—and recalls the words of the poet who compared one of her dearest characters—

"To some tall cliff that lifts its awful form,
Swells from the vale and midway cleaves the storm:
Though round its breast the rolling clouds are spread,
Eternal sunshine settles on its head."

At 5 o'clock on a clear, frosty morning, some three years ago, after having staged and horsebacked it some miles from Eatonville—one can go further by rail now—a party of seven, including the writer, started from Camp Muir, 10,200 feet above the level of the sea, on the final installment of our trip to the summit of the mountain. Our way—for path there is none—lay along what is called the Cowlitz cleaver, a ridge of rock which saparates the Nisqually glacier from the Cowlitz. The Cowlitz glacier is the fountain head of the Cowlitz river, which flows into the Columbia. The melting waters of the Nisqually glacier, on the other hand, form the Nisqually river, which winds its tortuous way to Puget Sound. The edge of the cleaver in parts is so sharp that two drops of rain falling a few inches apart would find their ultimate destination hundreds of miles apart. From Camp Muir our stiff climbing began, but nothing especially dangerous was encountered until Gibraltar rock was reached, a huge pile with basaltic base and topped by conglomerates rising eight hundred feet sheer out of the side of the mountain. While it may be millions of years since Mount Tacoma was a hole in the ground, its geological formation indicates that it is of recent growth compared with the age of the earth. We saw on its face conglomerates composed of different kinds of rock between the formation of which millions of years may have elapsed. The varying state on the top of Gibraltar indicates that it was once level with the surrounding plain or mountain, when one day the pent fires in the bosom of the earth burst forth and Mount Pelee was not in it with the fireworks that ensued. Above us was the rock, 800 feet high; below, the Nisqually glacier, a drop of a thousand feet, where a false step would send the unfortunate who lost his nerve or his footing to be dashed to pieces or to slide into one of the crevices that run across the glacier. Near the upper part of the rock the guide had to go ahead and chop steps in the steep wall rock and pass the lifeline down to the climbers. After an hour's hard work we passed the danger point and at 9 o'clock stood on the edge which rises over the rock and above the White river glacier, just four hours after we had left Camp Muir. Here we rested awhile to draw breath and gaze on the wild desolation of the glacier. Imagine a wide valley filled with a chaos of broken ice thrown together in wild confusion, like the ruins of a lost world. We could see the White river wend its way from its source, the valleys of Eastern Washington became unfolded to our gaze, and the elevations of the Summit mining district, which seem so level from Tacoma, looked rugged and seemed formed of a multitude of sharp pinnacles.

We left Gibraltar a few minutes after 9 o'clock for our last long pull to the summit. Here the light air began to affect some of our party. Some got sick at the stomach, while others had to rest at frequent intervals; in fact, about two hundred feet was as much as any one of the party could make without a rest, when they would stop exhausted and gasp for breath, and what seems most remarkable is the fact that, no matter how tired one was, one minute's rest would revive him. This is accounted for by some with the explanation that the breath gives out before the muscles get tired, and as soon as the breath returns one is as active and supple as ever. At 11:40 we reached the zone of rocks which surrounds the crater, and when the writer jumped on top and called for three cheers for old Mount Tacoma everyone was too tired to respond. Two hours were spent on the summit, part of which was occupied in writing letters to distant friends, dating them from the top of Mount Tacoma, or Rainier, as the taste or judgment of the writers would suggest. On the south side of the crater, protected by the wall of lava rock, the sun shone bright and warmed the rock and made it comfortable for all to sit and rest. Here the Rev. Mr. Pendleton, one of our party, conducted a short religious service, and the singing of grand old "Rock of Ages, Cleft for Me" on the ancient heights of Mount Tacoma, typical of the rock which shall endure forever, seemed singularly appropriate. We then crossed the crater to Columbia peak, the highest point on the mountain. Here the change of temperature was sudden and disagreeable. On the south side we were protected by the wall of rock, but on the north side there was nothing to shelter us from the icy wind, which blew through our whiskers like a blizzard on a Kansas prairie. My own hands got so cold that I could hardly hold my alpenstock. Here we found a small American flag which someone had placed in the solitude and snow. The day was perfect. Not a cloud obstructed our view. The Olympics and Cascades seemed like walls of stone built by giants. To the north rose Mount Baker, clear and bright, while over the British line Mount Scott was plainly visible, thus bringing to our view, as indicated by mountain peaks, the states of Washington and Oregon and the British province of British Columbia, the territory of the two greatest nations of the earth. The Puget Sound country seemed spread like a map before us, but so great was the area that this whole district, with its great and busy cities, seemed small in comparison. Tacoma was more distinctly visible than any other point on the Sound, partly on account of the great volume of smoke that rises from her many factories. After a stop of two hours, we prepared for the return. When all was ready, the life line was spread out and those who, like the writer, had not their footwear well provided with spikes, were placed in front, the surer-footed behind, and we started down the mountain. Like the famous six hundred who charged at Balaklava, we stopped for nothing. If one of the party slipped, he slid until he could regain his feet. It was a case of "Slide, Kelly, Slide." It took us just forty minutes to reach Gibraltar, from which point it had taken us two hours and forty minutes to ascend. Here we realized the need of a guide, for a slide had obliterated all trace of the steps we had cut in the morning. Fortunately a clump of ice stood up four feet or so high. Around this the guide passed the lifeline and lowered each one down to a place of comparative safety. It took the party one hour and ten minutes to pass this point, but it seemed like an eternity to most of us, as the hot sun was loosening the rocks on top, and the thought would present itself that they might come down any moment and blot the party out of existence. While at this critical point a fall of snow and rock on the other side shook the mountain, and a lot of rock was dislodged over our heads, but we were so close to the mountain side that the mass passed harmlessly over our heads and there was no immediate danger unless one of the splintered rocks above took a notion to fall. After getting safely past Gibraltar our way was comparatively easy and we made Camp Muir in just three hours from the summit, including the time spent at the danger point. Another half hour's rest and, rolling our blankets, we started for Reese's camp, making the five miles in an hour and a quarter, finishing one of the pleasantest and most memorable journeys ever accomplished by any of the party.

TACOMA'S SPLENDID PARKS

By E. R. ROBERTS, Superintendent of Parks.

One of the most striking proofs of the progress and refinement in our city is the rapid increase of taste for parks, schools, and homes, and ornamental gardening. It cannot be denied that the tasteful improvement of city homes, both of the rich and the poor, is both one of the most agreeable and the most natural recreations that can occupy a cultivated mind, and over appreciation of the beauty of natural scenery becomes frofounder and more sympathetic with what we fondly term the advance of civilization.

In 1907, men with clear heads and strong hearts are needed to cultivate good fellowship and maintain some common sense. Our system of public parks should be complete and as comprehensive as our highest knowledge and culture can make it; and only good can possibly come to any people whose goal in public education is continually advancing toward the highest ideals of modern times.

The true purpose of public parks is to provide for the dwellers in cities convenient opportunity to enjoy beautiful natural scenery and to obtain occasional relief from the nervous strain due to the excessive artificiality of city life. Tacoma ranks before all other cities for its natural style of parks: North, south, east and west of city centers—"Jerusalem was set in the midst thereof"—and it is noted for their large acreage. Tacoma has added to its park holdings over twelve hundred acres in the last fifteen years. The surface of these is most gracefully undulating. From each park the scenery is grand: Mountains, waters, islands, and valleys—the scene is extremely beautiful and striking, especially when you recall the true name of the grand old mountain, Tacoma, as seen from Tacoma's parks.

A list of the parks:

	Acres.
Point Defiance	638
Spanaway	380
Wright	26
McKinley	30
Lincoln's	45
Firemen's Park	1
Totem Pole	¼
Terry Park	½
Norton's	¼
South Second	¼
South Seventh (C to Commerce)	¼
North E (6th to 7th)	½
Parkway 66 ft. wide from Lincoln Park to Spanaway	86
Total	1,220

Point Defiance park is to Tacoma what the Golden Gate park is to San Francisco, or Central park to New York, the leading park, and always will be. The system commences here. One hundred and fifty thousand people were introduced to this beautiful woodland last summer. As the visitor enters, the natural scenery is extremely striking and beautiful, which leaves a perpetual impression. From the delightful bits of virgin scenery here, the vegetation supplies the best and most comprehensive indication of the character of the climate. Amid belts and groups and masses of evergreen trees and shrubs are winding walks stealing off, here and there, in the most inviting manner.

To the right the walks take the visitor seven miles

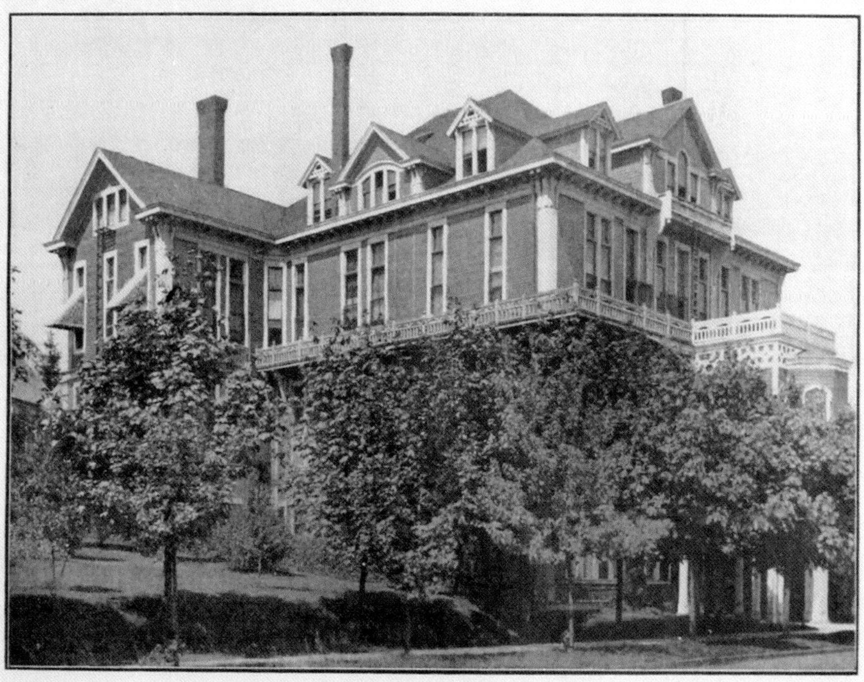

FANNIE C. PADDOCK MEMORIAL HOSPITAL.

The oldest and most popular institution of its kind in Tacoma is the Fannie C. Paddock Memorial hospital. It is charmingly situated immediately to the west of Wright park, and is in every respect a model and up-to-date establishment. Dr. Charles McCutcheon is now, and has been for a number of years, the physician in charge.

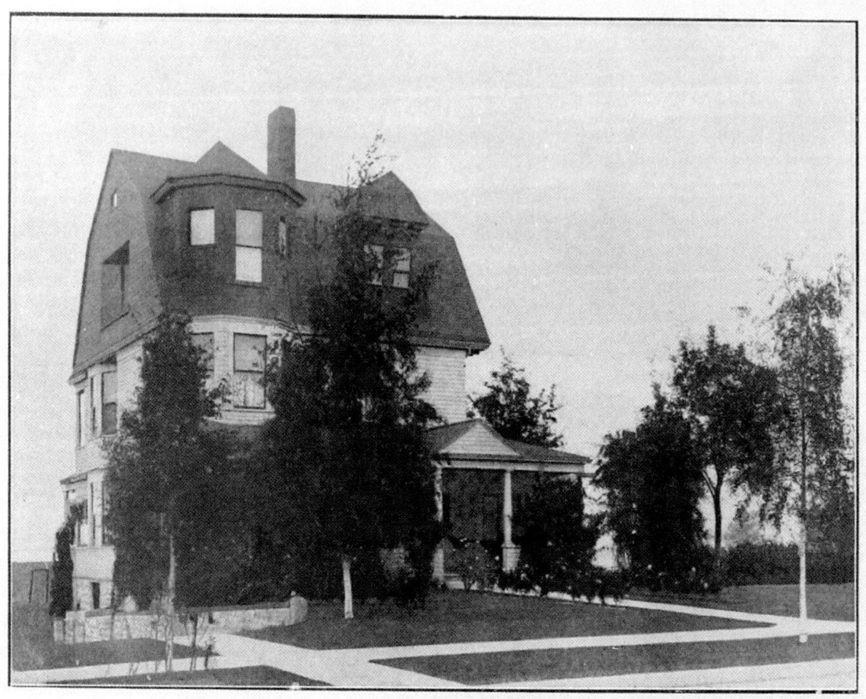

Avery. RESIDENCE OF B. D. CROCKER, U. S. INTERNAL REVENUE COLLECTOR.

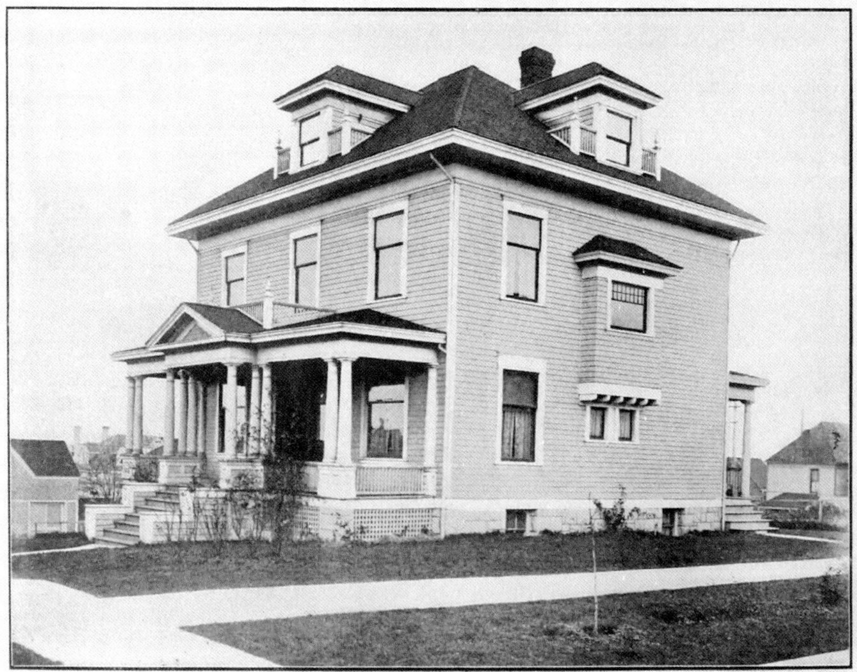

Avery. RESIDENCE OF LA GRANGE SMITH, PRESIDENT NORTH COAST STEAMSHIP COMPANY.

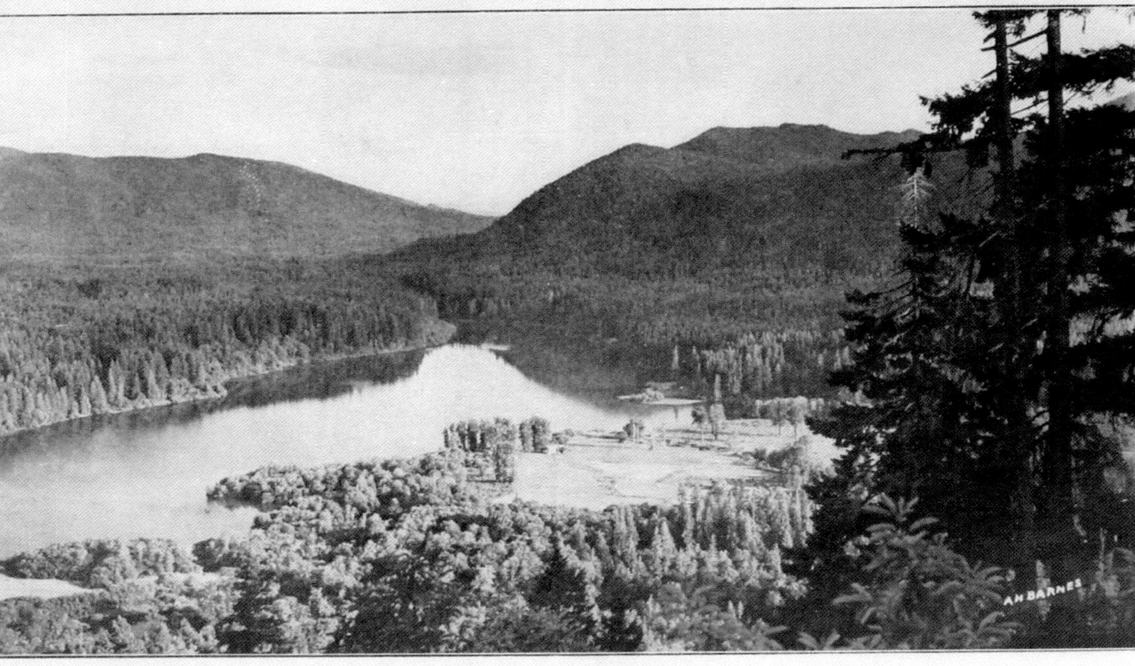

Avery.

LAKE CUSHMAN, IN THE OLYMPICS.

A Favorite Outing Spot—Photo Taken From a Point 2,000 Feet Above the Lake.

through a grand woodland park; the left walks bring the visitor to a park of rose bowers, a flower garden, a conservatory full of exotic flora, a water garden with nearly a hundred birds of many varieties, and the animal garden. Buffaloes, elks, deer, goats, bears, kangaroos—these last from Australia, the Melbourne botanical gardens. Two baby kangaroos were born since last September, each carried in the mother's pocket, from which it looks forth upon the delighted visitors, children and parents, with whom these animals are the latest favorities. There are foxes, wolves, raccoons, wild cats, monkeys and others. Eagles, with their grandly aloof glance over the heads of the curious, perch in solitary dignity, and manifold other birds go to make up an interesting collection.

Last year the park commissioners brought this park up to being one of the most prominent parks in the Northwest. Proper shelter and buildings were provided for the animals, giving a metropolitan look all in keeping with their surroundings. A bear court was built of rocks, cement and iron—there is no bear pit like it in the country. It cost $2,000, is very characteristic and will last for all time. There were 15,000 feet of water pipes laid and 15,000 feet of drain tiling. A reservoir and lake were constructed; a cedar arch at the southeast entrance gives dignity to the approach, which must be seen to be appreciated.

As the year is mellowing into autumn, with its indescribable, though somewhat pathetic, charm, we must not forget the keenest delight a spring garden brings. In anticipation of that resurrection of the year's life, while yet the gloom of winter's death was gathering, last fall over 50,000 bulbs were planted in the flower garden. There is no other city in the Pacific Northwest that has 50,000 bulbs planted in its park. To perfect all this work neither pains nor labor were spared. And the resultant surpassing beauty is the reward thereof.

Wright park is a remarkable instance of a large, beautiful acreage in the heart of a city. In that respect it is the most important park of all. Here the nursemaids and mothers take the children to play, and the student learns his Latin, lying the the grass, with the tall poplar rustling high above him, and the fountain splashing softly in the lake in the vale below, from whose leafy nooks peep statues of woodnymphs and fauns. Wright park has the greatest variety of trees, about 250 in variety in fact, and it is wonderful to observe how very many exotics are found there, proving that this climate is naturally adapted to their growth.

MUNICIPAL WORK IN 1906

Tacoma's Public Improvements Valued at More Than $1,000,000 For the Past Year

Municipal improvements amounting in cost to more than $1,000,000 were made in the year closing December 31, 1906, in continuation of the general system started in 1905. The principal expenditures for 1906 were:

Ten miles street paving, $600,000.

Nine miles grading, $90,000.

Twenty miles cement walks, $105,000.

Thirteen miles wooden walks, $30,000.

Fifteen miles sewer, $70,000.

South Tacoma trunk sewer, four miles, $60,000.

Twenty-two miles water mains, $120,000.

Total, $1,075,000.

Plans for this year are for improvements that will amount to as much as, if not more than, the work done last year.

The Standard Oil Company has established an independent agency at Tacoma, making this port the distributing center for all points as far east as Pasco and south as the Columbia river. The company has just completed a large plant on the tideflats, where large buildings and steel tanks, having a capacity of 2,000,000 gallons, have been erected. A pipe line extends from the tanks to the dock near the Northern Pacific drawbridge, so that oil steamers can discharge here. A fleet of steamers will be operated by the company between Port Point Richmond, where it has a large refinery, and Tacoma.

TACOMA CHAMBER OF COMMERCE

A Representative Organization That Is Doing Much Valuable Work in Advancing the Interests of the City

Among the commercial bodies of the Pacific Coast there is none that outrank the Tacoma Chamber of Commerce and Board of Trade as a broad-gauge organization, representative of the strongest and most progressive business and industrial interests of the community. In every movement calculated to advance the welfare of the city the Chamber of commerce has proven itself an influential factor. Its campaign of advertising Tacoma has been in recent years both comprehensive and aggressive, and as a result Tacoma is not only better known throughout the East than ever before, but is acquiring new population, increasing in industrial strength and extending its commercial influence in greater degree than any other city in the West. Never before in its history has the chamber been so strong numerically. Its present membership numbers 550. During the past year 210 new applications were received, with a net gain of 200 members. With it is affiliated the cream of Tacoma's progressive citizenship, and in the consideration of questions of public interest its influence is being directed with a fidelity to the welfare of the city that establishes its worth as a potent agency in the advancement of Tacoma. The organization is peculiarly fortunate in commanding the services of a man of tireless energy and high ability at the head of its executive department. Secretary Louis W. Pratt has demonstrated his eminent fitness for directing its affairs, and to his initiative and intelligent effort is due much of the splendid success that has been achieved during the past two years.

The headquarters of the Chamber of Commerce are located in a fine six-story structure, erected for its occupancy, and owned by the Tacoma Chamber of Commerce Building society. To the intending resident, investor or visitor a courteous welcome is always extended, and a mine of information is made available.

The annual elections of the chamber are held on the first meeting night in September. It is now officered as follows: President, Wm. Jones; vice-president, J. S. Whitehouse; treasurer, Geo. W. Fowler; secretary, Louis W. Pratt; manager traffic bureau, Ralph H. Hoitt; trustees, Henry Hewitt, Jr., Joshua Pierce, Wm. H. Dickson, R. G. Hudson, Geo. B. Kandle, Jesse S. Jones, A. V. Love, F. L. Kellogg, Wm. Virges, F. B. Woodruff, C. H. Plass, August Von Bocklin.

REAL ESTATE DEALS FOR 1906

They Treble Those of 1905, With Total Considerations Exceeding Twenty Million Dollars

The business in Tacoma realty deals during 1906 almost trebled that of the previous year and more than doubled that of any previous year.

The transfers aggregate in number 12,217 of a total expressed consideration of $20,274,135.

The nearest approach to that is found in the boom year of 1891, when the transfers aggregated in value $9,537,757.

For 1905 the transfers numbered 6,156, of a value of $7,770,075.

For 1904, the transfers numbered 6,806, of a value of $7,019,530.

For 1903, the transfers numbered 6,806, of a value of $4,646,537.

For 1902, the transfers numbered 6,862, of a value of $4,436,025.

Of course it is well understood that few of the deeds give the real consideration. If the actual conditions were carried in the deeds of last year, the value would probably approximate $60,000,000.

THE NORTHWEST METROPOLIS

By R. F. RADEBAUGH.

When we speak of Tacoma as surely destined to become the metropolis of the Northwest we mean to include a wide range of territory. The term is to be defined as embracing Washington, Oregon, Idaho, Montana, British Columbia and Alaska. The "metropolis of the Northwest" has been on the move, lo! these many years; but in coming to Tacoma, on the verge of the great ocean, it can go no further. It abides here and gives laugh to dreaming aspirants that have gone before. Cincinnati, away back in the Buckeye state, now accounted far East—pioneering scene of the elder Nick Longworth, our Alice's grandfather-in-law—was the metropolis of the "Northwest" of nearly three generations ago, and her newspapers of that time rang the changes upon her ascendant star and the happy and golden prospect. But her term of rule was of short duration, and her scepter fell away under the lengthening shadow of the giant of the lakes. Chicago became the metropolis of a greater Northwest lying beyond, and yet towers, higher and higher, as the seasons pass, trade center for teeming, multiplying millions—national emporium, indeed, world marvel among inland cities, and whose limits of expansion lie beyond vision of the true prophet.

Again, in the like direction, the width of two states beyond, northerly and westerly as the course of empire takes its way, the later "Northwest" pitched its tent at the Falls of St. Anthony, and there became builder of Minneapolis and St. Paul, twin cities, at the head of the Mississippi Valley, the commercial center of still another and more extended "Northwest," reaching to the summit of the Rocky Mountains. Minneapolis journals of twenty years ago, exalting and promoting, declared that their location seemed destined, from geographical, political, industrial, commercial and transportational considerations, to become the central metropolis of the continent—the future seat of North American empire. They quoted extensively some French Canadian, who, writing in a, then, current number of the North American Review, maintained that "continental union" was the ultimate destiny of Canada and the United States, and added the comment that Minneapolis would be the continental capital. Thus so wild, for inlanders, like noisy geese.

Next come we to a long step in the westward course. The process is again being repeated, this time for all the vast region north of 42 degrees which lies west of the Rocky Mountain range, the latest "Northwest," and the greatest, though not the last, for Alaska is left. The developments here, on the continental boundary at tidewater, facing the Orient in trade connection, with its many hundred millions, are destined to so far supercede and eclipse those of the twin cities that the latter will almost pass out of ken of the world at large when the name of Tacoma will be leading among the maritims cities, which are the greatest, and her fame ringing in the ears of all men from darkest Africa through Asia, Europe, America and the islands of the sea.

For, note the difference between inlander and seaport—and such a seaport! In addition to serving and taking profits as a trade center for adjacent and tributary country—and as to this function Tacoma is in prospect fully at par with, not only the twin cities, but also with Chicago, owing to the surpassing wealth of natural resources backing her—in addition to this, we say, Tacoma is located directly in the international and trade route and highway, chosen by nature's inflexible topography of upraise, rock and scarp—we may well challenge the world on this score; has the very best of all harbors, not a single exception admitted or worth listening to, though we respectfully listen; less than any other of port charges for ships calling here, and more suitable ground for a vast railway center and operations than any other Coast city of the Pacific ocean, or any ocean, on either side. (See Donald Fletcher's lucid, authoritative and able showing.)

Therefore, give us leave to say, and giving it not, we take it, willy-nilly, for we are absolute in this, our conviction, founded on the rock of Truth, that though the limits of Chicago's growth are beyond reach of the true prophet's vision, we are clear in the opinion that Tacoma will beat her in the next 25 years, maybe less. For smaller towns, we do not see them.

VALUE OF STATE'S DAIRY PRODUCTS

For Year Ending November 1, 1906, Output Approximates $5,000,000 — Pierce County, With 4,263 Cows, Produces 400,000 Pounds of Butter Annually

In round numbers, for the year ending Nov. 1, 1906, an aggregate value of $5,000,000 was the output from the straight milk sales, according to the biennial report of L. Davies, state dairy and food commissioner, recently completed. This does not include the output from 155 creameries for 1906, the reports of which have not been received by the commissioner.

Butter manufactured in the state during the year aggregated nearly 8,000,000 pounds, an increase of about 400,000 pounds over the previous year. Of this, 1,735,000 pounds were manufactured east of the Cascades, the remainder on the west side. For the year the state output of butter reported was 7,479,000 pounds, of which 1,934,000 pounds were from the east side. Commissioner Davies says that 155 creameries remaining to report this year probably will swell the total for the year to 9,500,000 pounds.

Pierce county, with 4,268 cows, produces in her creameries about 400,000 pounds of butter annually. Snohomish leads in number of dairy cattle, with 8,026 cows in 1905, but her production of butter was only about 900,000 pounds. Many of the cows near the centers of population are used almost exclusively to supply the milk routes and little of their product reaches the creameries.

In 1905, with 51,282 cows in the whole state, 241 creameries reported plants valued at $281,591, and a butter output of nearly 8,000,000 pounds, valued at $1,946,982.

In 1906 the 233 creameries that reported covered the product of 45,433 cows, aggregating 7,479,000 pounds of butter, valued at $1,969,000.

Spokane county, with thirteen factories, leads in cheese production with 120,428 pounds in 1905 out of a total state production of 547,000 pounds. They made 114,802 pounds this year.

The condensed milk output shows a considerable increase. The output in 1905 was valued at $442,088, and this year at $532,587. In the last two years condensed milk valued at about $800,000 was shipped away from Puget Sound and about $600,000 worth to Alaska. State creameries are getting a good proportion of this trade.

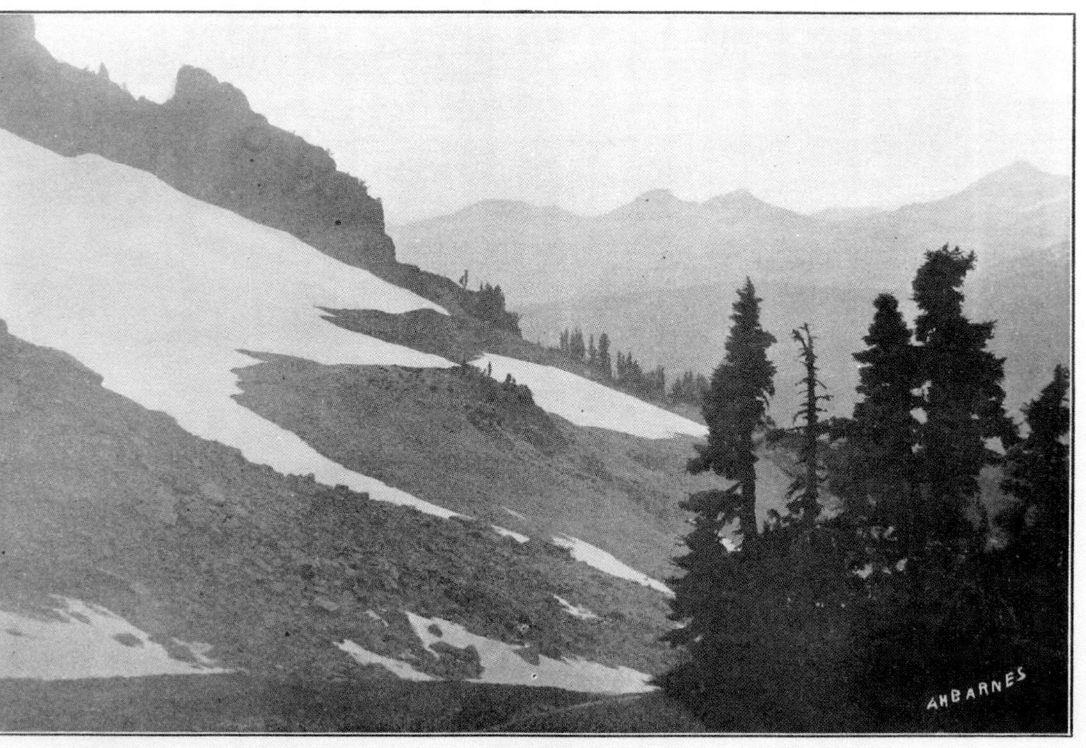

SNOW FIELDS ON NORTH SLOPE OF PINNACLE PEAK, TATOOSH MOUNTAINS.

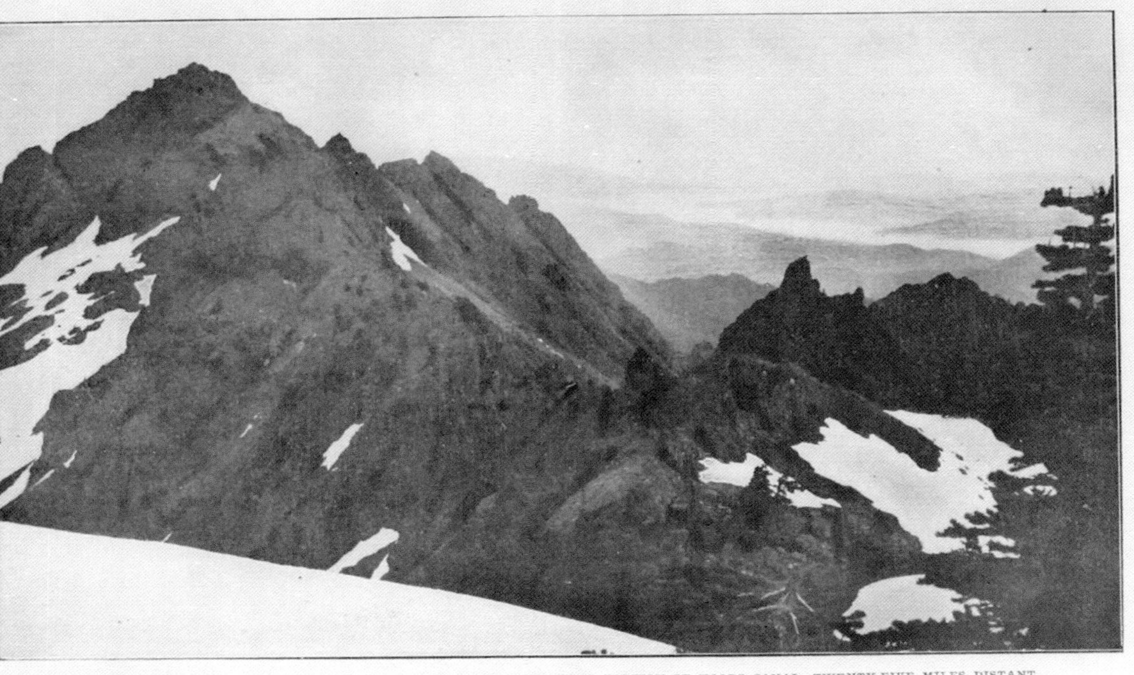

Barnes. NORTHEAST VIEW FROM MOUNT ELLINOR, OLYMPIC RANGE, SHOWING PORTION OF HOODS CANAL, TWENTY-FIVE MILES DISTANT.

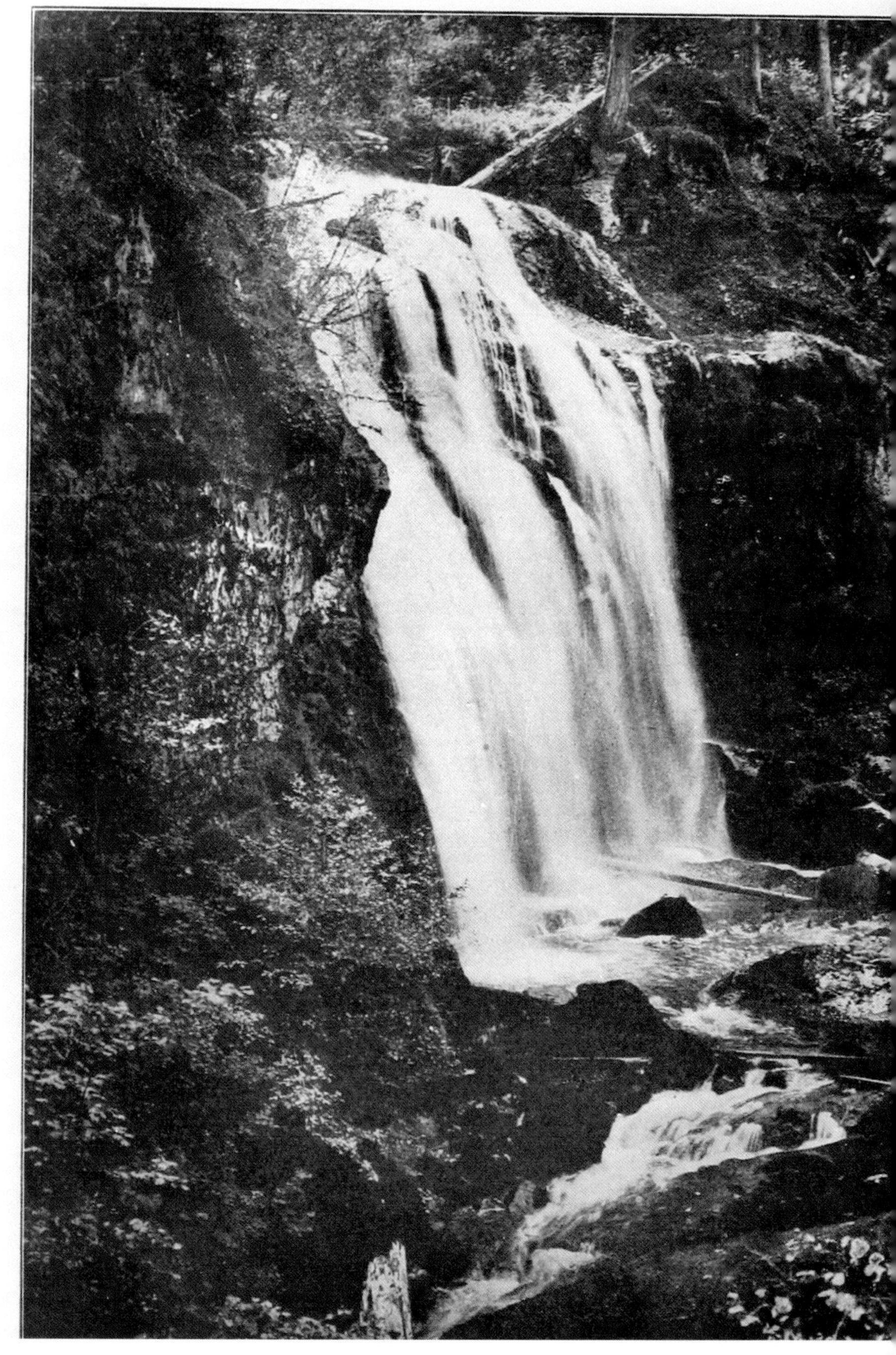

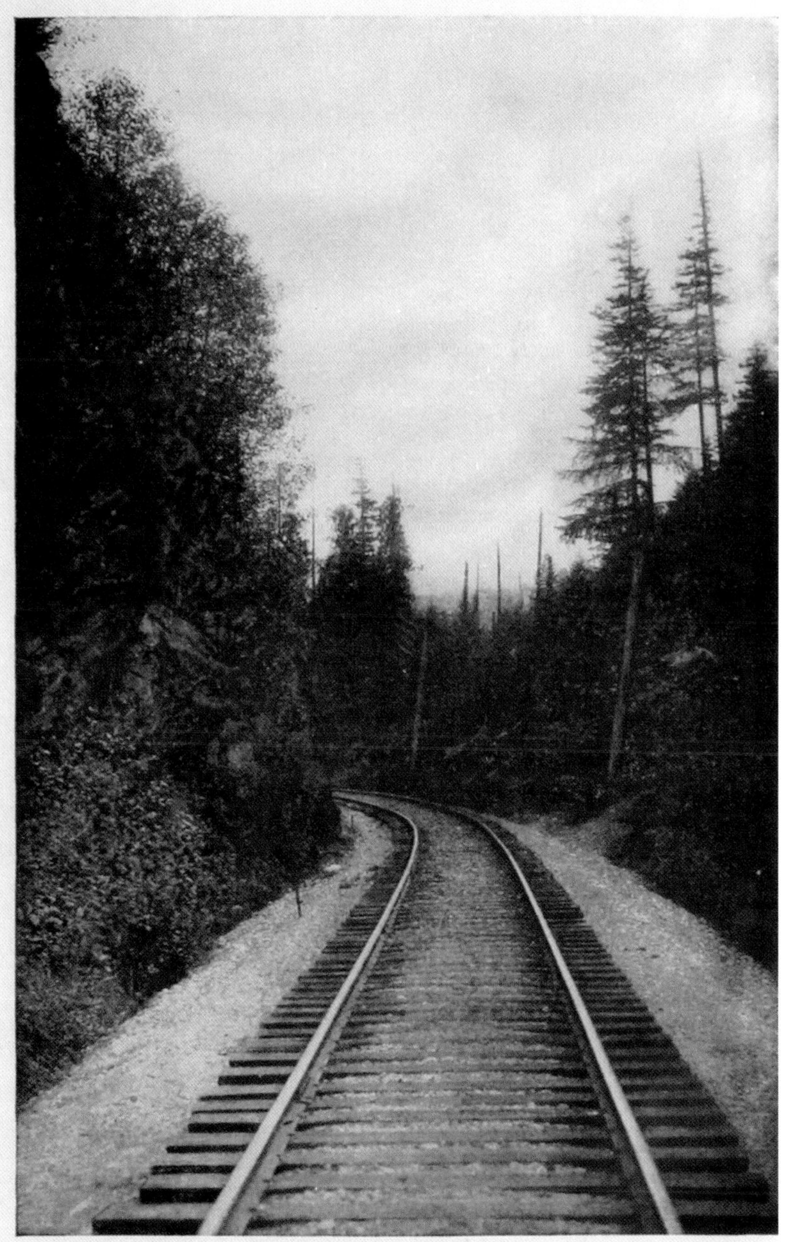

Wonderland. IN THE CASCADE RANGE.

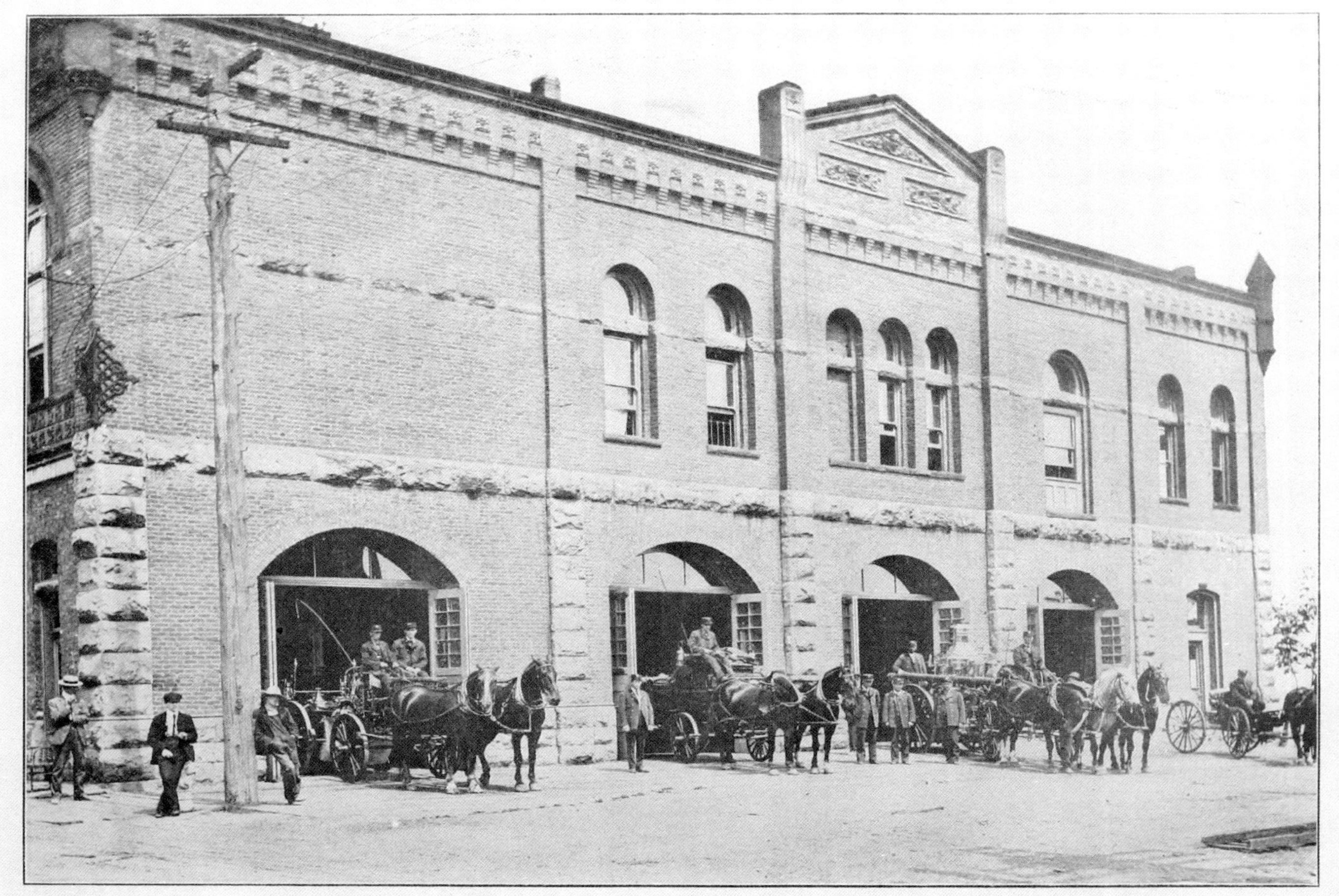

Avery.

HEADQUARTERS TACOMA FIRE DEPARTMENT, SOUTH NINTH AND A STREETS.

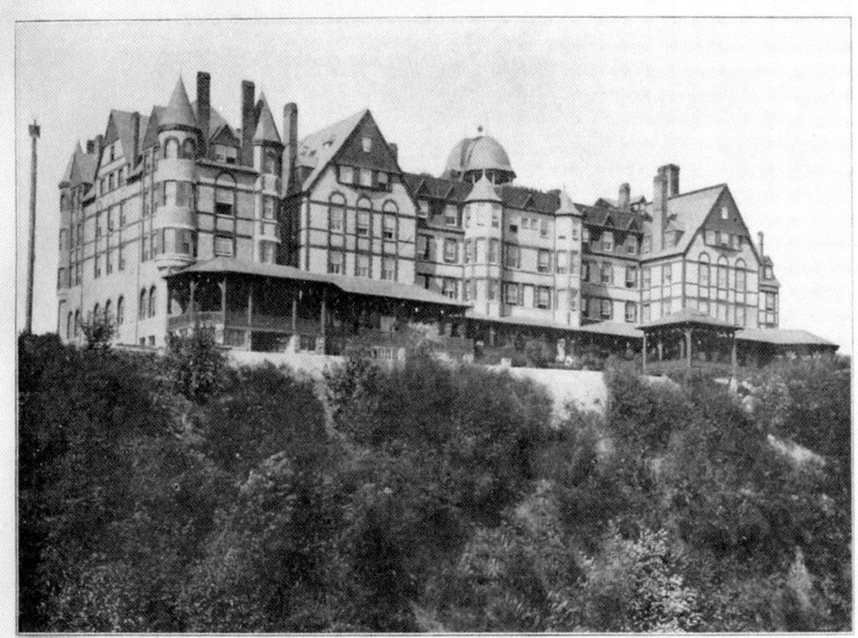

Avery.

HOTEL TACOMA

Newly remodeled at an expense of nearly $200,000. The Finest Hotel in the Northwest. Overlooking Commencement Bay. Bath Rooms supplied with Sea Water. Hot and Cold Water in every room. A modern and splendidly appointed Cafe.

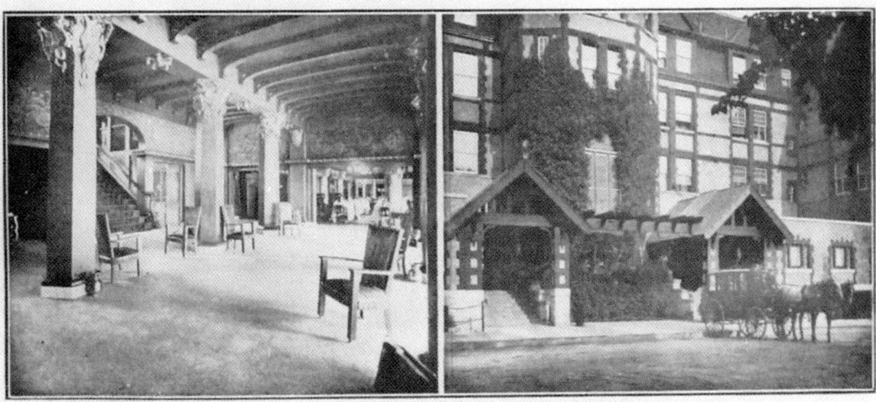

Avery. THE LOBBY. MAIN ENTRANCE.

OUR ADVERTISERS

To the tens of thousands in all parts of the United States, as well as abroad, who will examine the contents of the New Herald Annual for 1907 we commend, as a specially important feature, the advertisements of leading business men and firms which occupy a number of its pages. The list is one of which any high-class publication might well be proud, since it comprises none but those of high reputation and standing in the community, and hence in whom the outside public generally may have full confidence.

INDEX TO ADVERTISEMENTS

J. E. DOLSON

REAL ESTATE

If you are intending to invest in Tacoma or desire improved or unimproved city or country property, it will be to your advantage to call or write to me.

A General Real Estate and Mortgage Loan Business.

J. E. DOLSON

1 and 2 Columbia Bldg., over Postal Tel. Co. Main 311

TACOMA

THE METROPOLIS OF SEAPORTS

With four more Transcontinental Railroads under construction as fast as men and money can build them, heading for her unexcelled harbor, Tacoma will be indeed the Mecca for Investors in Tacoma Real Estate in 1907. Fortunes have been made in 1906, but 1907 will eclipse it many times. Are you going to be among the fortunate ones! Come, see, help Tacoma and your money grow—but you've got to hurry.

For further information, see or address

Otto B. Roeder

REAL ESTATE BROKER

OFFICES: 1201 PACIFIC AVENUE TACOMA, U. S. A.

RESIDENCES

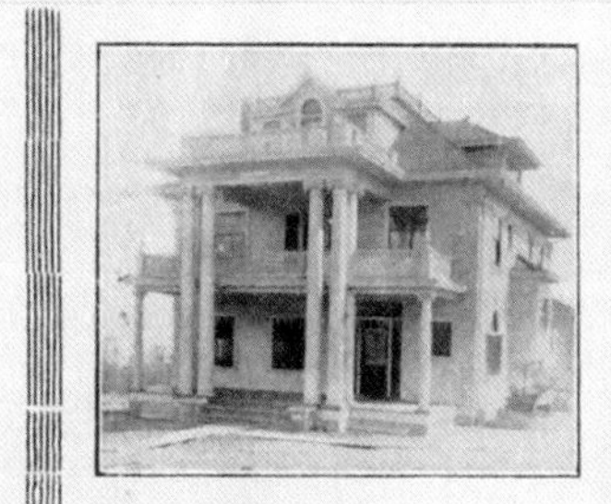

The adjoining cut shows one of the many beautiful homes which we have for sale in Tacoma. It has been built less than two years. It commands a magnificent view of the bay and the Olympic and Cascade Mountains, and of Mount Tacoma. Is situated on the best car line in the city. Four or eleven lots go with the place, at a price much less than it could be duplicated for at present prices of material and lots.

One-third down, balance five years. Five lots and eighteen-room residence, finished in hardwood, located three blocks beyond the retail district, on C street. Brings $125 per month rent. Buy now. Get benefit of five years' increase in value. Sell before final payment.

LOTS

$35 each, one-half down, buys high- level lots. Best of soil. Within walking distance of N. P. car shops. No one will deny that these same lots will bring four times the price within four years.

INVESTMENTS

Valuable business corner. Absolutely the best buy for the money on the street.

Tidelands for factory and mill sites.

Five lots, with trackage, close to business center.

All kinds of improved and unimproved real estate in and near Tacoma.

G. D. GRANT & CO.

504 Chamber of Commerce Bldg., Tacoma, Wash.

In making investments one of the most vital points is to buy right, and this is particularly true of Western Real Estate Purchases.

The Eugene Church Company, 501 Equitable Building, Tacoma, Washington, have earned quite an enviable reputation during the past few years on account of their success in managing sundry investment syndicates, for whom they are buyers and managers.

These syndicates are always handled in corporation form and certificates of stock issued to the various parties interested.

During the year 1906 several of these very successful investment companies have been organized by the Eugene Church Company, among which are the following: The Lakewood Land Company, capital paid up, $30,000; Pierce County Land Company, capital paid up, $20,000; Tober Land Company, capitalized for $25,000—40 per cent. paid; Suburban Land Company, with a capital of $1,000.

One of these companies has already paid dividends of 700 per cent.; but, of course, it is not usual to earn such dividends in so short a time, even in the far West. A number of syndicates composed of local business men do their buying and selling through the agency of this concern.

Mr. Eugene Church comes from New York and has been engaged in handling City and Suburban real estate in Tacoma for the last ten years, and has associated with him Mr. W. M. Wilson, former business manager of the Tacoma Daily News, and Mr. J. W. Moore, a former banker of Nebraska.

If you have any money to place in Western investments, you will make no mistake in dealing with the Church concern.

HENRY C. CHESEBROUGH, President.
JOHN W. CLASSEN, Secretary.
WILLIAM H. HANSON, Vice-President.
CHARLES E. HILL, Resident Manager.

San Francisco Office: 234 California St.
Cable Address: "Mahanson."

Annual Capacity, 150,000,000 Feet

Established 1868.

Tacoma Mill Co.

TACOMA, WASH.

LUMBER, SHINGLES, LATH, SPARS AND PILING

RAIL AND WATER SHIPMENTS

GENERAL MERCHANDISE

Eastern Representative
H. H. COLLINS
Lumber Exchange, Minneapolis, Minn.

FRANK GOUGAR, Pres. WM. F. RYDER, Sec'y. and Treas.

Ryder-Gougar Company, Inc.

CAPITAL PAID UP $25,000.00

REAL ESTATE AND INVESTMENTS

—AND—

GENERAL INSURANCE AND PROPERTY AGENTS

Choice list of property FOR SALE; also a number of fine homes FOR RENT constantly on hand.

LIST your PROPERTY with us. SATISFACTION GUARANTEED.

WE HAVE THE FINEST EQUIPPED OFFICES IN THE NORTHWEST

776 Commerce St., Cor. Ninth St.

Telephone Main 6003

TACOMA, WASH.

H. J. Schwinn & Co.

FINANCIAL AGENTS

ARCADE BLDG.

REAL ESTATE, LOANS AND FIRE INSURANCE

MORTGAGE LOANS A SPECIALTY

Special attention given to care of property for non-residents. If you have money to loan on first-class real estate security, we can place it for you at a good rate of interest.

CORRESPONDENCE SOLICITED.

Tacoma Real Estate

We say, without hesitation, there is no other city on the Pacific Coast which offers as safe and sure profit-making possibilities as Tacoma, the City of Destiny. Write us for "Reasons Why," free for the asking.

The Yakima Valley

Also offers a splendid field for profitable investment. The soil of the farming lands of the Yakima Valley is firm in texture, easily worked, and contains all the chemical elements essential to fertility.

Correspondence solicited.

The Rist=Jones Co.

Real Estate and Insurance

Provident Bldg - - Tacoma, Wash.

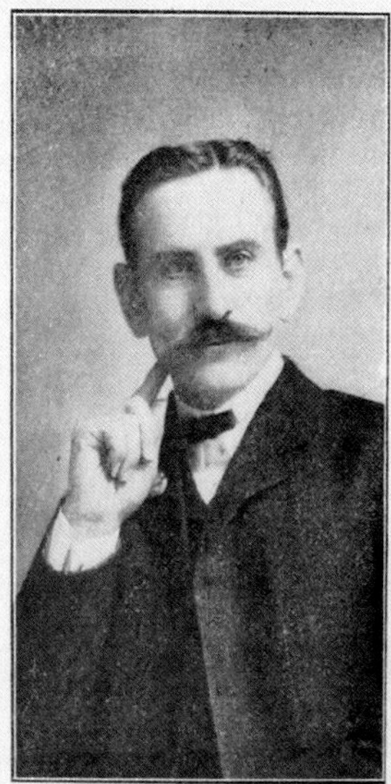

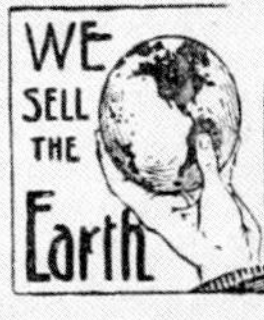

Real Estate
Loans
Rentals
Collections
City and Farm Properties

All matters relating to investments, the sale, purchase, care and management of property carefully attended to. Seventeen years' practical experience in this business in Tacoma. Reference, any bank in the city.

H. B. RITZ & CO.

FINANCIAL AGENTS,

600 National Bank Commerce, Tacoma.

25 years in Tacoma. 18 years in the Real Estate business.

For Investment

We have some of the very choicest City property that will net you a handsome profit. Bargains in Improved Farms and Suburban Property. We have some very fine Manufacturing Sites for sale, advantageously located.

Bertelson & Co.

REAL ESTATE, LOANS AND INSURANCE

Tide Lands for Sale

Houses Rented. Taxes Paid. Entire charge taken of property. References—Any Bank or Business House in Tacoma.

Rooms 3 and 4, 1308 Pacific Ave.,

TACOMA, WASH.

RENTALS LOANS

FOR SALE

NORTON & HILL

201-2 BERLIN BLDG.

REAL ESTATE INSURANCE

Property Surveyed and Located.

H. Robert Paul & Co.

Dealers in All Kinds of

REAL ESTATE

Acreage and Timber Lands a Specialty

ROOMS 311 AND 312 ARCADE BUILDING

Office Telephone, Main 5261 TACOMA, WASH.

PHONES: Office, James 586; Residence, Red 5957.

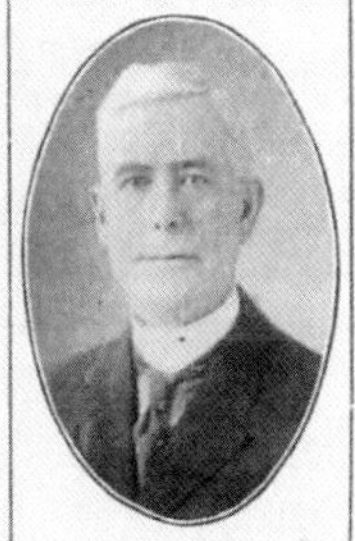

R. D. Shutt

Real Estate

Insurance

Collections

MONEY TO LOAN ON IMPROVED REAL ESTATE.

Special attention given to care and sale of property for non-residents.

320 BERLIN BUILDING, TACOMA, WASHINGTON.

JOS. SPARLING. JOHN SPARLING.

SPARLING BROS.

REAL ESTATE, LOANS, INSURANCE,

RENTALS AND COLLECTIONS

Property Bought, Sold and Cared For for Non-Residents.

213 Arcade Bldg., TACOMA, WASH.

ESTABLISHED 1890.

Malcolm E. Gunston Co.

REAL ESTATE, LOANS

INSURANCE

Especial care given to properties of non-residents and estates. We represent a number of investors and can get you offers for your real estate. Eastern and local references.

Second Floor Bernice Bldg. TACOMA, WASH.

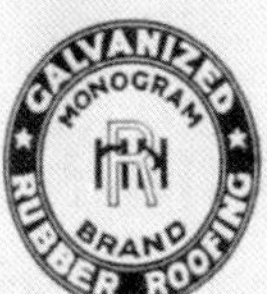
GALVANIZED
MONOGRAM
BRAND
RUBBER ROOFING

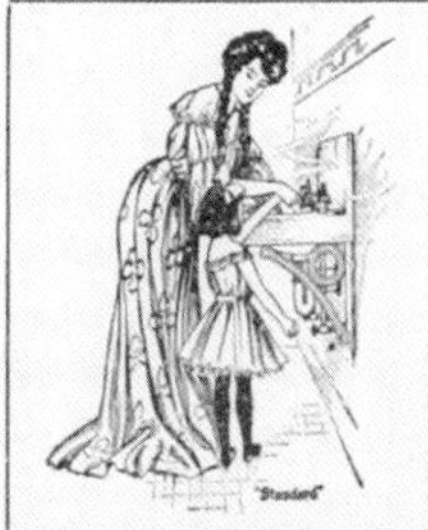
"Standard"

Phone: Red 1816.

H. B. Walter & Co.

REAL ESTATE AND LOANS

Many people in the past year have made from 50 to 100 per cent. on their investments. The same opportunity is open to you, and we will be pleased to show you properties that are sure to advance.

Houses Rented, Taxes Paid, Rents Collected.
FARM LANDS, TIMBER LANDS, TIDELANDS.
Business Opportunities.

WE PARTICULARLY SOLICIT EASTERN BUSINESS.

Entire charge taken of property for resident or non-resident owners. We give it our personal attention.

CORRESPONDENCE SOLICITED.

216-217 Arcade Bldg., Tacoma, Washington

ESTABLISHED 1886.

GEO. W. FOWLER

EQUITABLE BLDG., TACOMA, WASH.

REAL ESTATE, INSURANCE, MORTGAGE LOANS AND RENTALS.

The Care and Management of Property and Securities a Specialty.

Representing—
Continental Insurance Co. of New York.
Fire Association of Philadelphia.
Maryland Casualty Co. of Baltimore.
Combined Assets $27,447,043.18.

HIGH-GRADE INVESTMENTS
NETTING 5 TO 8 PER CENT.

Frank Snyder

CONTRACTOR AND BUILDER

105 NINTH ST.
TACOMA, - WASH.

Builder of the New Provident Block.

The Cow Butter Store

Makes a Specialty of

PURE AND HOME-MADE GOODS

We handle only—
Tacoma-Made ROGERS' BAKING POWDER
Tacoma-made BOTTLED MUSTARD
Tacoma-made VIOLET OATS
Tacoma-made CHOW-CHOW
Tacoma-made CRACKERS
Tacoma-made PICKLES
Tacoma-made CATSUP
Tacoma-made OLIVES
Tacoma-made HONEY
Tacoma-made LARD

THE PURITY OF OUR GOODS IS GUARANTEED BY THE MANUFACTURERS

TRY SPROULE'S TEA J. A. SPROULE, Prop.

M. SCHMIDT

MERCHANT TAILOR

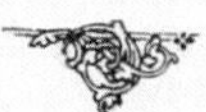

Imported English and Scotch Goods

TACOMA HOTEL

Telephone Main 950 Tacoma, Wash.

E. F. GREGORY CO., Inc.

REAL ESTATE, LOANS AND INVESTMENTS

Care of Property for Non-residents a Specialty

120 Twelfth Street TACOMA, WASH.

TELEPHONE, Main 229 P. O. BOX 205

COLUMBIA BREWING COMPANY

Brewers and Bottlers of

LAGER BEER
AND
PORTER

Try Our "GOLDEN DROP" Bottled Beer For Family and Table Use.

THE BEST ON THE MARKET

Nos. 2120-32 SOUTH C STREET

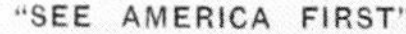
"SEE AMERICA FIRST"

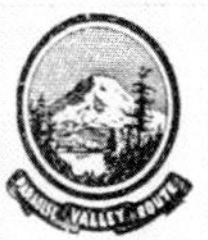

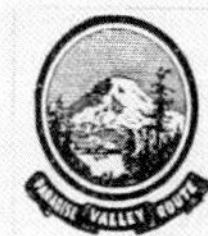

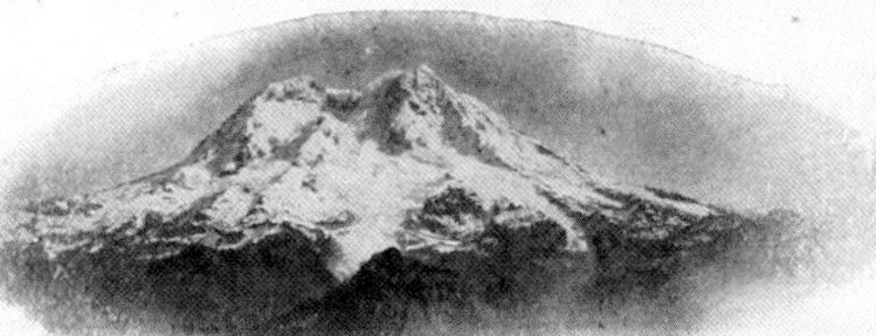

MT. TACOMA, IN THE "WONDERLAND OF THE CASCADES."

Reached Over the

TACOMA EASTERN RAILROAD

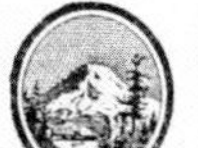

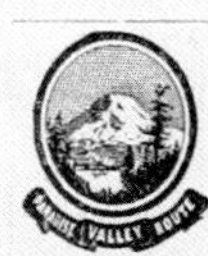

VISITORS TO THE NORTHWEST should not fail to see this indescribable region, with its grand volcanic, glacial peak, 14,528 feet high, 32,509 acres of perpetual ice and snow, 15 separate distinct glaciers, with yawning crevasses hundreds of feet deep, rugged canyons, beautiful waterfalls, magnificent forests and entrancing mountain parks, containing nearly 500 varieties of wild flowers that in season bloom within a step of perpetual snow. Good hotels and accommodations; reasonable rates. For free illustrated descriptive matter address

General Freight and Passenger Dept., Tacoma, Wash.

Electrical Supplies

Let us quote you in any quantity on anything in our line. We make prompt shipments and our goods are the best on the market.

We are in position to make immediate shipment on gas and electric fixtures at almost any price.

Stephens-Mullins Electric Co.

102 SOUTH TENTH ST., TACOMA, WASH.

"HIGH-GRADE LAMPS."

G. J. McPHERSON A. A. McAULAY

REAL ESTATE

LOANS AND INSURANCE

We can show the best Opportunities and Results for Investments of any City on the Coast.

WE BUY OF THOSE WHO WISH TO SELL

WE SELL TO THOSE WHO WISH TO MAKE MONEY

CALL OR WRITE FOR INFORMATION

McPHERSON AND COMPANY

609 Provident Bldg.

The People's Store

Under New Management

Tacoma's Largest Department Store

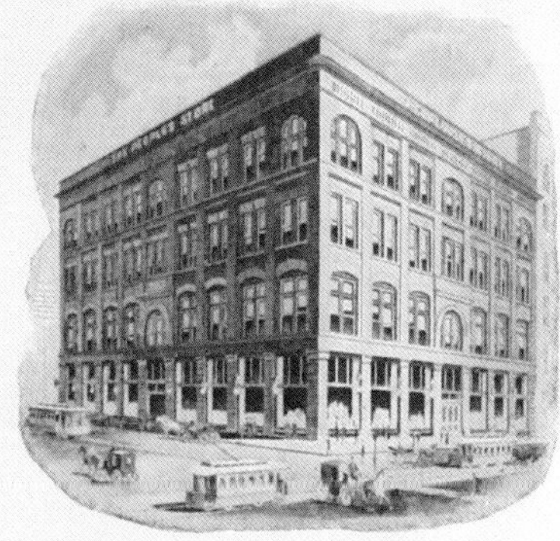

Thirty departments under one roof—each department a complete store in itself. With our mammoth Basement Bazaar we have five immense floors containing over 65,000 square feet of floor space.

"The Brightest Corner in Tacoma"—so called from the hundreds of Nearnst lamps recently installed, both on the inside and outside of the building, making it the lightest and brightest store on the Pacific Coast.

The interior of the building is now being refitted — new show cases and fixtures are being added, and the public will find here everything to please the eye and add to their comfort while buying or visiting.

Corner of Pacific Avenue and 11th Sts. : **TACOMA, WASH.**

1105 A Street
Tacoma.

411-415 Globe Bldg.
Seattle.

F. T. Crowe & Co.

Wholesale Dealers
and Agents in all kinds of

Building Material

Expanded Metal System of Fireproof Construction a Specialty. Johnson Bars for Reinforcing Concrete.

ALSEN'S PORTLAND CEMENT

The Strongest, Finest Ground and Most Uniform Cement Made in the World.

U. S. GYPSUM COMPANY'S
IVORY WOOD FIBER PLASTER

CORRESPONDENCE SOLICITED.

121 Munroe Street
Spokane.

252 Oak Street
Portland.

SHERMAN-CLAY & Co.

"THE HOUSE OF QUALITY"
And the
SUPREME - UNAPPROACHABLE

Steinway Piano

have for nearly half a century been closely identified one with the other.

We are proud to concede to this artistic piano the greatest credit for our success and standing among musical people and in the business world.

Our convenient new store is the outcome of a desire to give those who wish the Steinway, opportunity to see and test

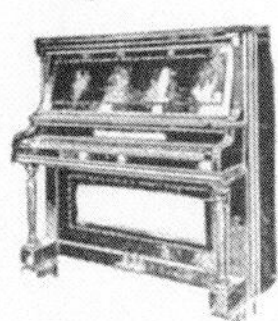

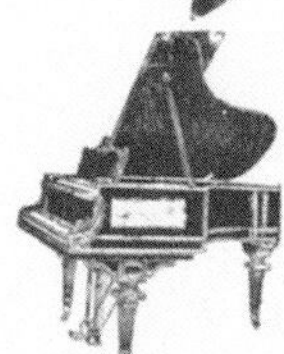

EACH AND EVERY STYLE OF
UPRIGHT, MINIATURE AND BABY GRAND
IN OUR TACOMA STORE

Tacoma's growing population will support such an effort, and we note a musical atmosphere here that demands it and we have met the need.

The Steinway is highest in price and most economical to buy, because years and years of continual use has proved its wonderful durability and perfectness of tone.

BESIDES THE STEINWAY
WE HAVE MANY OTHER MAKES

TACOMA STORE, 936 C STREET

SAN FRANCISCO
For 35 years—Corner Kearney and Sutter Sts.

PORTLAND — SEATTLE — OAKLAND
SPOKANE — EVERETT — BELLINGHAM